The
PENTATEUCH

Other Titles by W. H. Griffith Thomas

Genesis: A Devotional Commentary
Outline Studies in Matthew
Outline Studies in Luke
Studies in Colossians and Philemon
The Apostle John: His Life and Writings
The Apostle Peter: His Life and Writings
Christianity Is Christ
The Holy Spirit
Sermon Outlines on Christian Living

The pentateuch
The Historical books
the wisdom books
the major prophets
the minor prophets

The PENTATEUCH

Chapter by Chapter

by
W. H. Griffith Thomas

Foreword by
R. K. Harrison

Introduction by
Warren W. Wiersbe

Preface by
Winifred G. T. Gillespie

KREGEL PUBLICATIONS
Grand Rapids, Michigan 49501

The Pentateuch, by W. H. Griffith Thomas. Foreword by
R. K. Harrison; Introduction by Warren W. Wiersbe; Preface by Winifred G. T. Gillespie. © 1985 by Kregel Publications, a division of Kregel, Inc., P. O. Box 2607, Grand
Rapids, MI 49501. All rights reserved.

Library of Congress Cataloging-in-Publication Data

Thomas, W. H. Griffith (William Henry Griffith),
   1861–1924.
   The Pentateuch.

   Reprint. Originally published: Through the Pentateuch,
Chapter by Chapter. Grand Rapids, Michigan: Wm. B.
Eerdmans Pub. Co., 1957.
   1. Bible. O.T. Pentateuch—Commentaries. I. Title.
BS1255.T52   1985   222'.106   85-10076

   ISBN   0-8254-3833-0 (pbk.)

3 4 5 6 7 Printing/Year 94 93

Printed in the United States of America

CONTENTS

FOREWORD

Each era has its gifted interpreters of the Holy Scriptures, and W.H. Griffith Thomas must be reckoned among that elite group of authoritative expositors of God's Word in the twentieth century. A man of brilliant intellect, enormous energy, and profound Christian faith, he could write such definitive textbooks as *The Principles of Theology* on the one hand, and deeply devotional studies of various parts of Scripture on the other.

He was never more lucid, however, than when he was writing for such periodicals as *The Christian*. He had apparently planned to deal with every book of the Bible chapter by chapter, in successive issues of that publication, but was not spared to complete that task.

The present volume contains the articles on the Pentateuch, which have been edited by his daughter. They are models of simplicity and clarity that contrive to conceal very cleverly a massive erudition and spirituality. The first two chapters will prove of particular value to the beginning Bible student as they point out the proper way to study the Word of God.

As *Through the Pentateuch* unfolds, the reader is confronted consistently with the message of redemption and revelation through divine grace, and each chapter furnishes an opportunity for meditation on some aspect of that broad message. The era during which Dr. Griffith Thomas wrote was one of intense, and sometimes destructive criticism of the Holy Scriptures. Though he was acquainted with this situation, the author remained uncontaminated by its negative tendencies as he expounded the spiritual principles of God's Word.

The reader is thus furnished with a concise and accurate account of what the Pentateuch contains and teaches, and is given ample opportunity to reflect upon the significance of these ancient writings. To modern western readers the old Pentateuchal laws and rituals are often bewildering, but Dr. Griffith Thomas explains them with great skill, and by periodic references to the New Testament points out their significance for Christian living today.

As one who now teaches at the college where the author was once a professor, I can commend this lucid and uncomplicated analysis of the Pentateuch most warmly to all Bible students.

Bishops Frederick and Heber Wilkinson   R. K. HARRISON
professor of Old Testament, Wycliffe College,
University of Toronto.

INTRODUCTION TO THE AUTHOR

His advice to young preachers was, "Think yourself empty, read yourself full, write yourself clear, pray yourself keen—then enter the pulpit and let yourself go!"

William Henry Griffith Thomas (1861-1924) followed that counsel himself, and in so doing, he became one of the spiritual giants of his day. As a preacher and a teacher of preachers, he excelled in spiritual depth, practicality, and a simplicity of expression that made the most profound truths come alive with excitement.

His mother was widowed before he was born, and family financial demands forced him to leave school when he was fourteen. He was converted to Christ through the witness of some friends on March 23, 1878. The next year, he moved to London to work in an uncle's office.

But Griffith Thomas was determined to get an education, so from 10:30 p.m. until 2:30 a.m. each night, he gave himself to serious study. He became a lay curate in 1882, while attending lectures at King's College, London; and was ordained in 1885. Griffith Thomas belonged to that early fellowship in the Anglican Church that was unashamed to be called "Evangelical."

The day he was ordained, Griffith Thomas was admonished by the Bishop of London, William Temple, not to neglect his Greek New Testament. The young minister took that word to heart and, for the rest of his life, read one chapter a day from the Greek New Testament! This kind of devotion to God's Word shows up in his writings.

He ministered at St. Aldate's, Oxford, and St. Paul's, Portman Square (London), and in 1905 was named principal of Wycliffe Hall, Oxford, the Evangelical center for Anglicans studying for the ministry. He lectured there for five years, then moved to Toronto to join the faculty of Wycliffe College, where he taught for nine years. He and his family then moved to Philadelphia and Griffith Thomas entered a wider ministry of writing and Bible conference work. He was associated with some of the leading preachers and conference speakers of his day and often spoke at the large Bible conferences.

He joined with Lewis Sperry Chafer and others to found the Dallas Theological Seminary and was to have lectured there; but his death on June 2, 1924, interrupted those plans.

Back to the Bible Broadcast
Lincoln, Nebraska

WARREN W. WIERSBE

EDITOR'S PREFACE

Among the books of my late father for whose publication or reprinting I have had any responsibility, this volume has for me a very special poignancy, and for two reasons. First, it represents his last important writing, for he was engaged in its preparation during the months immediately preceding June 1924 when God took him Home; and it was I, as his secretary in that period, who made the original typescripts. Second, since the material took the form of a connected commentary on Bible chapters for daily reading that appeared in a weekly magazine, *The Christian* (of London), it goes forth now virtually as it came then from the pen that was so soon to be laid down, and without the need that sermon notes have for interpretation and reproduction. Throughout the work on it, therefore, I have felt at times that I could almost hear my father's voice. The dates of the readings, moreover, have held significance for me as I noted, for example, what message from him was appearing in print on the very days of his last illness, his death, and his funeral, and even on subsequent family occasions during those first months of sadness and loss.

There was, of course, a point in the file of clippings at which announcement of death was made, after which the author was designated as "late" and tributes were paid. The then Editor of *The Christian*, Dr. J. W. Thirtle, who had initiated the series of readings, wrote as follows:

> For many years past Dr. Thomas has been a contributor to the columns of *The Christian*. From his curate days at Oxford down to the very end of life, he was conscious of a sympathetic hearing whenever he had anything to say to readers of this paper. It was, therefore, with strong assurance as to his trustworthy guidance in regard to the things of faith that we approached him some months ago in reference to the weekly page of Bible readings which for long years have been an important feature of *The Christian*. Dr. Thomas saw in this ministry a great opportunity to bring back to the Book many who have a sincere desire to know the will of God; and from time to time during recent months his personal letters to us have been full of hopefulness that great results might accrue from this, his last strenuous undertaking.

The Notes thus supplied to our columns, under the general title of "Through the Word," have met with an enthusiastic reception; and we have witness, borne by ministers at home and missionaries on the field, that they have been effectual in promoting a veritable revival in Bible study . . . We rejoice to know that he was not unaware of the spiritual fruit thus granted to his labors . . . He was greatly stirred by the news, as he proceeded with characteristic diligence to combine spiritual enthusiasm with his fine equipment as a Christian scholar, ever with the aim of implanting in the hearts and minds of men and women a saving and sanctifying knowledge of the sacred Scriptures . . . We rejoice to believe that his example of devotion to truth, and his diligence in service, with the eminent success achieved, are likely to tell, not only among clergymen and ministers, but also among others who endeavor to show themselves "approved unto God," workmen "that need not to be ashamed, rightly dividing the Word of truth."

It is to Dr. C. T. Cook, a more recent Editor of *The Christian,* that I am indebted for the preservation of the file of clippings. His collection was virtually complete, which our own, for some reason, was not. Thus, without Dr. Cook's ready co-operation in supplying the material this volume could not have appeared, and so I am most grateful to him.

It was to have taken some three or four years for my father thus to go "Through the Word," and he proposed to use this general title for the publication of the entire manuscript in book form. Since, in God's inscrutable Providence, he was permitted to go no further than the middle of the Book of Joshua, it is only "Through the Pentateuch" that I can provide the chapter studies, together with his introductory material. Yet, as with other writings of his, I pray that these also may bring a fresh blessing in this day and to this generation, even as they have to me.

WINIFRED G. T. GILLESPIE

1

THE STUDY OF THE BIBLE
GREAT PRINCIPLES AND METHODS

THE BIBLE has three characteristics: it embodies a divine Revelation, and on this account it conveys a divine Message, and carries a divine Authority. It has been given to us for three specific purposes: historical information, doctrinal instruction, and spiritual inspiration. For all these reasons it calls for study. We ought to know its revelation, heed its message, and submit to its authority. It is essential to become acquainted with the nature and measure of its contents, with the material and meaning of its teaching, and with the substance and purpose of its message.

The value of an adequate knowledge of the Bible is obvious to all. Intellectual profit is derived from its information and instruction; moral profit from its guidance and warning; and spiritual profit from its doctrinal and experimental truth.

It will, therefore, easily be seen that knowledge presupposes much more than reading; it calls for thorough study; and not for study only, but also for a genuine and constant application of mind, heart, and conscience to the teaching of Holy Writ. We ought to realize the need and importance of as thorough and detailed a knowledge of the Scriptures as our time and capacity will afford. Bible study involves hard work because it demands thought. It cannot be accomplished by reading only, for Bible reading is not Bible study.

It is also far easier to read books about the Bible than to study the Bible for ourselves, for this makes far less demand on time and thought; but direct Bible study is at once the most essential and most profitable of our duties.

TWO GREAT PRINCIPLES

In our study of the Bible, there are two great principles which must ever be kept in view, first separately, and then together.

I. THE BIBLE SHOULD BE STUDIED LIKE ANY OTHER BOOK.

This means that we should endeavor to become acquainted with it, getting to know what it contains, and it implies nothing short of actual mastery of the contents. We may proceed along two distinct, yet connected, lines.

THE TELESCOPIC METHOD

1. The first of these has been called *the telescopic method*. This may be described as the endeavor to obtain "a bird's-eye view" of the Bible, a knowledge of books and portions, rather than of texts. It is often said that a man is in danger of not seeing the woods for the trees, meaning that he is so intent upon particular trees that he is unable to appreciate the beauty and proportion of the trees as a whole which form the woods. In the same way, it is only too possible to concentrate attention on words and texts and fail to see the larger aspects of God's Word.

For this reason it is necessary and important to master each book by itself. God has given the Bible in separate, though connected books, sixty-six in number, and we shall be doing what is at once the most natural and also the most helpful thing by endeavoring to master each book.

Perhaps there are three questions to be asked as we approach a book. *What? When? Why?* That is, we must see what the book contains; try to discover something of the date and circumstances of its issue; and then do our utmost to gather the precise meaning and message of its contents. For this purpose we shall be well advised to read a book straight through at once, in order to obtain a general view of it as a whole. Then it will be well to do the same again, without stopping unduly to attend to details. A third reading in this way will be most profitable, especially if at the same time we endeavor to make our own analysis of the book. When we have gained our own impression of what the book is and contains, then, and not till then, we may compare the results of our reading with those of some writer.

THE BOOK METHOD OF STUDY

The book method of Bible study will prove singularly fruitful. As an example of what may be done in this way, let us turn to the book of Genesis. A general reading will show that there are two main divisions, the first covering chapters 1 to 11, and the second, chapters 12 to 50. The former covers thousands of years, and may be summed up in five words: Creation, Corruption,

Deluge, Deliverance, Dispersal. The remaining thirty-nine chapters deal in detail with the lives of a few men, and five may be said to cover practically the whole: Abraham, Isaac, Esau, Jacob, Joseph. From this mere outline it would be possible to proceed to the thorough study of the contents of the fascinating first book of the Bible.

Or take Isaiah. The first thirty-five chapters deal mainly with Assyria. Then come four chapters of history, followed by twenty-seven chapters dealing mainly with Babylonia. It is noteworthy how the first two chapters of the history (36 and 37) look back over the first period, while the other two chapters of the history (38 and 39) look forward over the second period. This summary can be further divided into smaller sections, and the whole book thereby be mastered.

Look at Matthew's Gospel. The key is to be found in two passages, each containing the phrase "From that time" (4:17; 16:21). Everything before the former is introductory; then, between the two, we have our Lord's preaching without a single reference to His death; but from the time of the latter of these texts, He began to tell His disciples what would happen. Thus, we may think of Matthew's Gospel as giving to us the preparation (1:1-4:16); the proclamation (4:17-16:20); and the passion (16:21-28:20).

John's Gospel is also capable of thorough study by itself. There are two main divisions connected by the phrase "His own." The former covers chapters 1-12, dealing with "His own" who did not receive Him (1:11). The latter covers chapters 13-21, dealing chiefly with "His own" who did receive Him (13:1).

The book of Acts is also capable of thorough mastery by itself. There are two chief sections. The former with Jerusalem as the center (1-12) and the latter with Antioch (13-28). But it is interesting to notice that each of these is marked by sub-divisions, indicative of periods in the history of the Church, when the writer was able to summarize results up to a certain point. Thus, in chapters 1-12, we have summaries at 6:7, 9:31, and 12:24. In chapters 13-28 there are summaries at 16:5, 19:20, and 28:31. Then, too, it can be seen that the entire book is built upon the ideas suggested by the geographical extension of the Church mentioned in 1:8. Nor is it possible to avoid noticing that the first section of Acts includes five parts, dealing with Peter and ending with his imprisonment, while the second section has also five parts, dealing with Paul and ending with his imprisonment.

The Epistle to the Ephesians is also helpfully studied along the lines of its two divisions, chapters 1-3 being concerned with doctrine, and chapters 4-6 with duty.

Galatians is similarly capable of careful consideration along three lines, each taking two chapters: chapters 1 and 2, personal; chapters 3 and 4, doctrinal; chapters 5 and 6, practical.

These are only the barest hints of what can be done by this method of book study, and it should be said again that this is the most obvious, and, in many respects, the most fruitful way of becoming acquainted with the contents and meaning of the Bible.

SECTIONS AND DIVISIONS

In addition to the study of books, and side by side with it, it is possible to give special attention to sections of books, and, thereby, to become thoroughly acquainted with particular portions. Thus, we can study the great section of Isaiah, chapters 40-66, by noticing its three divisions of nine chapters each, for it will be found that at the close of chapters 48, 57, and 66, the same thought is recorded, though the second and the third times are in an intensified form. It is thought by some that even these nine chapters can be further subdivided into three times three. It is also worth observing that the former portion of Isaiah, chapters 1-35, is simply and naturally divisible into three parts: chapters 1-12; chapters 13-27; chapters 28-35.

As an instance of the study of sections in the New Testament, reference may be made to the Epistle to the Romans, and attention concentrated on the three pivots of truth found at the beginnings of chapters 5, 8, and 12, the word "therefore" referring respectively to the "therefore" of Justification, the "therefore" of Sanctification, and the "therefore" of Consecration.

Yet again, it is possible to pay special attention to the historical periods found in the Bible, inasmuch as the revelation of God is marked in this way in its development. Thus, we can look at the pre-Abrahamic period, covering the first eleven chapters of Genesis. Following this is the Patriarchal period, including the remainder of that book. Then comes the Mosaic period, extending over the life of Moses from Exodus to the end of Deuteronomy. Afterwards we have the period from Joshua to Samuel, dealing with the important period of the Judges.

The time of the first three kings, Saul, David, and Solomon, offers another natural section for study. Then the time of the divided kingdoms comes next, and attention can be given to either Israel or Judah separately or the two simultaneously. The periods of the captivity and the post-captivity complete the Old Testament. Similar divisions can be made in studying the record in the New Testament.

UNITY OF SCRIPTURE

ONE OF THE MOST essential and fruitful methods of becoming acquainted with the Bible is by the study of its connections and spiritual developments. The unity of the Bible is a very important topic. The Old Testament finds its unity in the three great offices of Prophet, Priest, and King. The need of a Priest can be seen very specially in the period covered by the books of the Pentateuch, though, of course, it is not exclusively associated with these. The call for a king is gradually heard as the historical books are studied from Joshua onward, while the importance of the Prophet is particularly visible in the prophetical books. And so, from Genesis to Malachi, the people show in one way or another the necessity of these three great features in regard to spiritual need.

When we turn to the New Testament, we find something very like the answer to these desires in the Person and Work of our Lord. In the Gospels He is recorded in His human life as "Jesus"; in the Acts He is seen in His divine power and authority as "Christ"; and in the Epistles He is especially revealed in connection with the Church as "Lord." Thus, "in Jesus Christ our Lord," we have the satisfaction sought by Israel when they desired a Prophet, a Priest, and a King. Jesus, the Prophet; Christ, the Priest; and the Lord, the King; the Prophet to reveal, the Priest to redeem, and the King to rule.

PROGRESS OF DOCTRINE

Side by side with this manifest and beautiful unity is the complementary truth of the Progressiveness of Divine Revelation. Starting with the early dawn in Genesis, there is a gradual development of light and truth until we reach the noonday in Christ.

Once again, we may look at the great outstanding truths of Scripture, as they are brought before us in the various parts. Thus, if we pay attention to Israel, we naturally find ourselves concerned with historical truth. If we study the sacrifices and offerings of the Old Testament, we are concerned with redemptive truth. If we ponder the various utterances and books of the prophets, we are face to face with prophetic truth. If we give attention to the life and conduct of the people, and notice the various aspects of morality enjoined and ordered, we become occupied with practical truth. So also in connection with the New Testament the various aspects are equally clear. In all this, whether with the Old Testament or the New, we may study with great advantage and profit, what may be called dispensational truth, expressive of the various ways and times in which God has revealed His will to man, from the earliest days in Genesis to the closing scenes in the Revelation.

THE MICROSCOPIC METHOD

2. The second line of study is often termed *the microscopic method*. This means attention to the details of Scripture, instead of to large sections or long periods.

a. Passages will naturally claim first consideration and as one out of many illustrations of the value of careful study of small sections, attention may be drawn to Psalm 63 with its fourfold emphasis on "my soul" in verses 1, 5, 8, and 9 — expressive of four different aspects or stages of the believer's life.

b. From passages it is possible to descend to verses, and very often a verse will yield a remarkable fulness of teaching when thoroughly considered. Thus in Acts 26:18 we see the whole Christian life starting with forgiveness and extending through sanctification to the glory that is to follow.

c. Biographies are often most profitable, not merely those which are recorded at great length, but also those of which very little is said. In the latter cases, careful arrangement and comparison of passages will often yield illumination. For example, it is not always noticed that the various texts connected with Mary, the mother of our Lord, show six connected stages in her spiritual growth.[1] The Apostle Barnabas can also be studied along five lines.[2] The characters of men like Nicodemus, with a very scanty

1. See the author's *Outline Studies in the Gospel of Luke*   (Kregel, Publications, 1984), p. 33.

record, can, nevertheless, be clearly seen in relation to Christ when the passages are put together.

d. The study of Bible phrases is also most fruitful, as illustrating this microscopic method. As one instance, the title "God of Peace," is often found in various connections, and shows something of the fulness of the Divine Character. In the Fourth Gospel, the words "in My Name" or "in His Name" will be found full of meaning. These are only bare illustrations of a wealth of teaching.

e. The words of Scripture are also fraught with wonderful power. No one could study the various passages where "grace" or "love" occurs, without obtaining remarkable insight into the truth of God. Then, too, a careful consideration of "justification" will reveal the sevenfold aspect of Scripture on this subject. Those who know their Greek Testament will find word-studies of immense value; e.g., the word "boast" occurs in seven different connections, and shows the profound distinction between the boasting which is wrong and unworthy and the boasting which is right and profitable.

One thing more should be said in connection with these methods of study; namely, that we shall find it worth while to use our pen in making notes, for this will at once clear our thought and help us to record the results of our work. Let it be said again that nothing less than thorough mastery will suffice, if we are to know our Bible. It has often been said that while justification is by faith, a knowledge of our Bible can only come by works.

II. THE BIBLE SHOULD BE STUDIED AS UNLIKE ANY OTHER BOOK.

Hitherto we have been concerned with methods of study which for the most part are common to all books, but it is important to remember that, as the Bible is in some respects unlike other books, it has to be studied accordingly. We cannot treat the Bible merely as any other book, because, notwithstanding its similarities, it is most certainly, and it claims to be, different. It claims to be inspired, and, therefore, the true way is to treat it as such. This will at once show its uniqueness. Other books for the most part are content to provide knowledge, but the Bible goes beyond knowledge and calls for obedience. We are thus

2. See the author's *Outline Studies in the Acts of the Apostles* (Wm. B. Eerdmans Publishing Co., 1956), pp. 105, 213-218, 296.

reminded that information alone is not sufficient; we must go forward to meditation. How, then, are we to study the Bible along this special line?

1. Each one must ask himself the question: "What does the Bible say to me?" This is the special point of Psalm 119:11 — "Thy Word have I hid in my heart, that I might not sin against Thee." One constant and real danger in the life of the believer is that of reading the Bible "for others." Preachers are constantly thinking of their congregations, and teachers of their classes; and in so doing we fail in the primary requirement, the application of the Bible to our own soul. It is imperative that we should constantly keep in mind this thought of the personal message of the Bible to the soul, and say: "What saith my Lord unto His servant?" "Speak, Lord, for Thy servant heareth."

2. In order that this may be so, the Bible requires three things from every true reader and student: attention, intention, and retention. The mind must first give closest possible attention. Then the will must put into thought and deed what the Bible contains, putting into practice what the mind has learned, in order that there may be definite results. And, meanwhile, the memory must keep in mind what is being taught, so that the Bible may continue to be the standard of living day by day. Thus, we may sum up the requirements once more as including Consideration, Meditation, and Application.

3. But it is perhaps necessary and important to look still more closely at this subject of personal Bible study and meditation along Scriptural lines.

a. We must search the Scriptures (John 5:39). The truth of the Bible is not always or necessarily found on the surface, and we must, therefore, go deeper and "search" to the utmost of our power.

b. Then will come meditation (Ps. 1:2). The Scripture, having been searched, will necessarily be applied to our own life, and meditation has been well defined as "attention with intention," emphasizing the reality and practical power of the thought we derive from the Bible.

c. Then will follow the need of comparison (1 Cor. 2:13). Scripture will be compared with Scripture, and we shall be enabled to see from time to time the variety, balance, fulness, and completeness of the spiritual teaching.

4. Descending still further into practical details of this essential method of Bible study, the following points call for special attention:

a. It must be *daily,* whether in the morning or in the evening, or at night. The Bible must be to the soul what food is to the body. "I have esteemed Thy words more than my necessary food."

b. It must be *diligent.* There must be no mere dreaming, musing over Scripture, but a thorough consideration and search in order to obtain "light and leading."

c. It must be *direct.* No second-hand messages will do; and however much we may value and rightly value the teaching of others, we must first and foremost have our messages direct from God Himself, and continually ask what Scripture says to us apart from others.

d. It must be *definite.* The purpose of this method of study is severely practical, and is intended to affect and transform our life. Whether, therefore, we are faced with a counsel, or a promise, or a warning, or an encouragement, or an example, we must seek to make it our own, and see that it has its right influence upon our life.

e. Then, when our Bible meditation is thus daily, diligent, direct, and definite, it will also be *delightful.* Like the Psalmist we shall say, "How sweet are Thy words to my taste!" "I rejoice at Thy word as one that findeth great spoil." Like the Prophet Jeremiah we shall testify, "Thy words were found, and I did eat them; they were to me the joy and rejoicing of my heart" (Jer. 15:16).

It is impossible to exaggerate the importance of this aspect of Bible study. Not only is it the secret of spiritual power in personal character, but it is the source of all blessing and of influence over others. Indeed, we may go so far as to say that the springs of all Revival, individual and collective, are to be found in the silent places of life. It is not without point that the Day of Pentecost came after ten days of waiting on God. Our Lord Himself had His times of quiet for meditation and prayer, and it is striking that, in the busy life recorded in Mark's Gospel, there are no fewer than ten occasions on which He went aside for communion with His Father. The same is true of the Apostles in their Christian life, for in proportion as they went alone with God they came forth with renewed vigor and power.

One of the reasons, surely, why our lives are often so superficial is that we are not enough alone with God. If Tennyson is right in saying that "solitude is the mother-country of the strong," we who are Christians will never be "strong in the Lord and in the power of His might" if we do not take time, and even make time, to go apart with Him in meditation upon His Word. The great preacher's little boy unconsciously explained the secret of his father's power in the pulpit when he told someone that "Daddy always talks with God in the study before breakfast." This is what the Psalmist meant when he said, "The law of his God is in his heart; none of his steps shall slide" (Ps. 37:31).

2

AN INTRODUCTION TO THE OLD TESTAMENT, NEW TESTAMENT, AND THE PENTATEUCH

THE BIBLE CONSISTS of sixty-six books, and yet they are really one in all essential features. Our English word "Bible" in the singular comes from a Greek word meaning "the books" in the plural, and as a record of the Divine plan of redemption, it possesses a unity from first to last which expresses the Divine purpose. This revelation of God was progressively given along two lines. First came the revelation of sin, its fact and consequences. Then followed the revelation of redemption, its provision and characteristics.

The Bible as we have it consists of two parts: the Old Testament, recording God's preparation, both of the Redeemer for the world, and of the world for the Redeemer; and the New Testament, with its provision of the Redeemer and the manifestation of Him in the life of the Church, and the prospect of His rule over the world. Taken together, these two parts are a complete record of God's method of salvation.

I. THE OLD TESTAMENT

The Old Testament consists of thirty-nine books, written by at least thirty authors, and covering at the lowest estimate one thousand years. It consists of history, law, poetry, philosophy, and prophecy, and is an Eastern book with a progressively-given revelation. In view of the fact that it comes from the East, it is not surprising if it is often found difficult of comprehension in the West; and many parts of the Old Testament become quite clear when Eastern life is understood. The Jewish division of the Old Testament consists of three parts. (1) The Law, or the five books of Moses. (2) The Prophets: these are called "former" and "latter." The "former" prophets are descriptive, and are what we understand as history, Joshua, Judges, Samuel, and Kings. The "latter" prophets are what we understand as prophecy proper, and are largely predictive. They consist of Isaiah, Jeremiah, and Ezekiel, with the twelve Minor Prophets.

(3) The Writings. This section includes the remainder of the Old Testament, in this order: Psalms, Job, Proverbs, Song of Solomon, Ruth, Lamentations, Ecclesiastes, Esther, Daniel, Ezra, Nehemiah, Chronicles. The order of the books in our English version is from the Greek translation of the Old Testament, known as the Septuagint, and consists of four main divisions: Mosaic, Historic, Poetic, Prophetic.

The Old Testament is God's revelation in its earlier and incomplete form, and consists of two stages. First, the introduction of God's revelation to the world through Israel, as recorded in the five books of Moses, the Pentateuch. Then, the progress of that revelation in the life of the nation of Israel, preparatory to the coming of the Messiah. This aspect covers the rest of the Old Testament, thirty-four books. The purpose of the Old Testament in general is to lead to Christ (John 5:39, 46; Luke 24-27, 44). It has been computed that in it there are over three hundred predictions, and that in the New Testament there are over six hundred quotations from the Old. Then there is a personal aspect of the purpose, for the Old Testament was written for our sakes (Rom. 4:23, 24), our learning (Rom. 15:4), and our example (1 Cor. 10:6, 11). See also 2 Timothy 3:16, 17.

II. THE NEW TESTAMENT

As a building to its foundation, so is the New Testament to the Old Testament. It is the completion and crown of all that is there foretold. It consists of four main parts: (1) The Gospels; (2) The Acts; (3) The Epistles; (4) The Revelation.

In the Gospels we have the life of Christ, which is the foundation of Christianity. In the Acts we see the commencement of the building of a Church on that foundation. In the Epistles we notice the provision of instruction for the Church. And in Revelation everything is crowned by the anticipation of the future triumph of Christ and His people, over all opposition. Thus, in these four sections we have the biographical, historical, practical and prophetical elements of God's complete revelation, and at every point "Christ is all."

As God's revelation has been given to us in book form, it is supremely necessary to study, and, as far as possible, master the contents and theme of each book.

III.   The Pentateuch

The five books of the Pentateuch record the introduction of the Divine religion into the world. Each book gives one phase of God's plan, and together they constitute a real unity. Genesis speaks of the origin of the religion, and of the people chosen by God as its medium. Exodus records the formation of the people into a nation, and the establishment of God's relationship with it. Leviticus shows the various ways in which this relationship was maintained. Numbers shows how the people were organized for the purpose of commencing the life of the divine religion in the Promised Land. This book also tells of the nation's failure and the consequent delay, with re-organization. Then Deuteronomy shows how the people were prepared, while on the border of the Promised Land, for the entry which was soon to follow.

As to the human origin of the Pentateuch, the conclusion to which we are brought through an ordinary reading of it is that Exodus, Leviticus, Numbers, and Deuteronomy are indeed of Mosaic authorship, while Genesis is indubitably of Mosaic editorship. It is highly probable that Moses compiled it from preexisting documents or books, under the inspiration of the Holy Spirit. There are sixteen chapters in Exodus and in Numbers, and twenty in Leviticus, that begin with "And the Lord spake unto Moses," or some equivalent expression, while Deuteronomy is full of similar phrases; but, naturally enough, in all of Genesis Moses' name nowhere appears. This is, of course, because the very latest event mentioned therein had occurred, at the shortest estimate, more than half a century before the birth of Moses, and the preceding human history covers a period extending to more than two thousand years of a prior antiquity. Indeed, the book of Genesis covers about one-half the history of the world, or a period roughly equivalent to that which separates the Exodus from today.

3

THE BOOK OF GENESIS

INTRODUCTION[1]

I. The Title

The King James Version follows the Septuagint and indicates the contents by the title, taken from the first word of the book in Hebrew, Beginning. This characterization is true of the entire book, for it is one of genetic development throughout.

II. The Purpose

Genesis nowhere records its own purpose, but by careful reading it is possible to grasp its unique significance, for it is indeed the record of several beginnings. In particular, it tells first of the beginning of the world, the period from before Adam to Abraham, and then of the beginning of the Covenant People of God, the period from Abraham to Joseph. These two epochs are seen in the two main divisions of the book: chapters 1 to 11, with its brief summary of the world's history (primeval); and chapters 12 to 50, with its elaborate detail about only four men (patriarchal). The first division is introductory to the Hebrew history in the second.

Abraham is the central figure and most of the contents of the book concern him and his posterity. We may stand, as it were, at chapter 12 and first look back at Abraham's descent from Adam, and then look on and survey his descendants. Or, we may say that eleven chapters are devoted to heaven and earth, and thirty-nine to Abraham and family. If this seems like a disproportion it is in reality the key to the purpose of Genesis. The book could have begun with Abraham if the Hebrews were an ordinary race, since Jacob was the real founder of the Twelve Tribes and Abraham could be mentioned merely as his grandfather, according

1. For a much more detailed treatment of this book, see the author's volume *Genesis: A Devotional Commentary* (Wm. B. Eerdmans Publishing Co., 1945).

to a common procedure of the modern biographer. But the Hebrew race is not an ordinary one, and the wonder is that chapters 1 to 11 are included at all — not that they are so fragmentary. This is another way of saying that Genesis is not the universal history of mankind, but the unfolding of the divine purpose of Redemption and how it was to be accomplished. It is history with a special purpose, namely, to set forth as the foundation of the Biblical religion the origin of the divine plan of Redemption, and also the origin of the people chosen as its depository. The religion of the Bible is shown to be the bringing back of man to God through Redemption, and all its dispensations and developments were designed to this end.

III. THE PLAN

The literary structure of Genesis is clear and simple. It is divided into an Introduction and ten sections each headed "These are the generations" or "The book of the generations," as follows:

(1) Introduction (1:1 to 2:3).
(2) Heaven and earth (2:4 to 4:26).
(3) Adam (5:1 to 6:8).
(4) Noah (6:9 to 9:29).
(5) Sons of Noah (10:1 to 11:9).
(6) Shem (11:10:26).
(7) Terah (11:27 to 25:11).
(8) Ishmael (25:12-18).
(9) Isaac (25:19 to 35:29).
(10) Esau (36:1 to 37:1).
(11) Jacob (37:2 to 50:26).

These show that the book consists mainly of a compilation of family documents. Pre-existing materials were used by the author or editor (cf. Luke 1:1-4), traditionally Moses (cf. N. T. corroboration, e.g., John 1:45; 5:34), and welded into unity in a truly masterly way. It is thus that Genesis traces the antecedents of the Chosen People and of the Messiah.

There is also a rational and spiritual as well as a literary plan, in three main sections:

(1) Introduction: The Origin of the Religion of Redemption as connected with the Creation of Man (chaps. 1 and 2).

(2) The Fall of Man and its Consequences (chaps. 3 to 11).

(3) The New Beginning (chaps. 12 to 50).

Dr. G. Campbell Morgan has appropriately described these three sections as Generation, Degeneration, Regeneration. Or we may call them Construction, Destruction, Reconstruction. True throughout to the idea of "beginnings," Creation begins with a view to human development. Sin begins by showing its power over human life, and Redemption begins in primeval promise to mankind and is presented in preliminary symbols.

IV. THE UNITY

There is thus a definite literary and religious unity in Genesis, however it has come about. It should, therefore, be studied as a whole. There is an exact chronological thread running through it, and all parts of it are interdependent. There is also a similarity of language throughout and, like the remainder of the Pentateuch, it is written in accordance with a definite plan worked out consistently from beginning to end. It is this unity that gives each book its literary form and stamps the group as the first known examples of a literary conception of history.

There is a regular series of genealogies from Adam to Jacob, occasionally interrupted for the introduction of related facts, and then resumed. They deal first with collateral branches of Adam's family before the main topic of Israel is introduced, e.g., Cain before Seth, Ham and Japheth before Shem, Terah before Abraham, Ishmael and Esau before Isaac and Jacob. The apparent tacks and turns are strictly in accordance with the fundamental principle of "beginnings," and thus Genesis is full of "geneses."

God's presence is prominent throughout and it is shown how, under His guidance, the purpose of Redemption was accomplished by the separation of the chosen man and the chosen race from others, and how they were fitted for carrying out that purpose. A characteristic sign of unity is the law of selection. The section 1:26 to 11:32 gives the Abrahamic descent and explains why a new start became necessary, and why Abraham was chosen from among the sons of Terah even as Seth, Noah, and Shem had been chosen before him. The reason why such a selection was necessary is shown to be the perennial conflict of good and evil.

Another way of regarding the unity of the book is to observe that it records the story of man, not of creation in general. Who

are the great men, the representative men of Genesis? Each of
them is connected with an event, a threefold promise and a sign.

1. Adam - in whom the race was born:
   a. Event: Fall - sin;
   b. Promise: threefold - conflict, victory, suffering;
   c. Sign: Cherubim and sword - separation through sin.

2. Noah - in whom the race was preserved:
   a. Event: Flood - judgment;
   b. Promise: threefold - dominion, sanctity of life, assurance;
   c. Sign: Rainbow - separation because of sin.

3. Abraham - in whom the race was blessed:
   a. Event: Call - redemption;
   b. Promise: threefold - land, seed, blessing;
   c. Sign: Circumcision - separation from sin.

Thus we see three themes in all this: sin, judgment, redemption; three men, events, promises, signs; and in each case the
promise answers to the need: Savior, safety, blessing. Man is
fallen, punished, redeemed; God is Creator, Judge, Savior.

V. THE VALUE

Genesis is the foundation of Biblical revelation and the explanation of all that follows in the history of Redemption through
the Seed. There is no truth that is not here in germ. Its completeness also is noteworthy. When the calling of Israel is
properly appreciated the sweep of chapters 1 to 11 is the more
evident, in all its moral breadth and grandeur. It is a pre-
Jewish book, human, universal. Looking back from Jacob, it
ever widens in view until Adam; while on from Jacob there is
an ever-widening-out in fulfilment of the divine purpose.

Thus Genesis should be studied not merely as history, but as
a succinct record of some of the stages in God's effort of mercy
to restore man to righteousness. Only thus may we understand
its omissions and inclusions. It should be studied in constant
view of the presence of the supernatural element. God is in
Genesis for Redemption, and this fact constitutes the difference
between it and all other books dealing with what is known as
primitive religion. It should be studied as part of a volume
that is in truth the Word of God, a fact that gives it its authority.

It cannot be accounted for unless acknowledged as an integral part of an inspired volume.

VI. THE MESSAGE

The Keynote of Genesis is the first four words of 1:1, "In the beginning God." It is thus a book of divine beginnings. It shows the origin of Creation, Man, Sin, and Redemption, with special emphasis on Redemption, and as such its message is four-fold:

1. God's Presence. The prominence of God in chapter 1 is seen throughout. He is the Creator, Lawgiver, Preserver, Judge, Redeemer.

2. God's Purpose. Redemption is dominant from first to last, affecting the selection and proportion of materials.

3. God's Plan. This is carried out —
   a. Under His own guidance. All through it is "God first." Man is the instrument, not the agent.
   b. With a definite object. This is not civilization (Cain), not conquest (Nimrod), but the spiritual blessing of salvation (Abraham).
   c. Through suitable instruments. God works through means and His instruments must be fitted to His purpose. The supreme requirement is faith, as seen in Noah, Abraham, Isaac, Jacob, Joseph (cf. Heb. 11:6). The unfit are eliminated, from Cain down to Reuben. There must be faith to respond to God's revelation.

4. God's Promise. From first to last this is the support and nourishment of His people. It has been well said that Genesis commences with God (1:1) and ends with a coffin in Egypt (50:26); but while this is true we must not forget that the coffin was associated with Joseph's absolute assurance of God's visitation according to His word (cf. 50:25), and was expressive of strong faith and certain hope.

Thus, through God's Presence, Purpose, Plan, and Promise, Genesis looks forward to a great future, culminating in the Apocalypse (cf. Gen. 1 to 3 with Rev. 20 to 22 and note the corresponding particulars). *Genesis* is to be transformed into

Palingenesis, when human generation is succeeded by super-natural regeneration, through Him who is both the Seed of the Woman (3:15; Gal. 4:4) and the Deliverer out of Jacob (49:10; Rom. 11:26).

CHAPTER STUDIES

Genesis 1

THE STORY of the Creation.

Verse 1 is introductory, emphasizing God as Creator. The sub-stantive "God" is in the plural, while the verb "created" is in the singular. This breach of grammar is also seen in 1 Thessalonians 3:11, and suggests a fulness in the Godhead, and perhaps a hint of what afterwards was developed in the doctrine of the Trinity.

Some think that verse 2 refers to the results of the fall of Satan and of vast geologic changes, and render the word "was" by "be-came." See Isaiah 45:18. The rest of the chapter would then record the renovation of the earth, and its preparation for man. Note the two adjectives in verse 2, "without form" and "void," or "formless" and "empty." Then the six days are divided into two triads, the one referring to the first adjective, how the earth re-ceived its form, and the other to the second, how the fulness came to be. This can be seen better if the six days are listed in parallel columns:—

Form	*Fulness*
First day: Light	Fourth day: Lights
Second day: Air	Fifth day: Fowls
Second day: Water	Fifth day: Fish
Third day: Land	Sixth day: Animals
Third day: Plants	Sixth day: Man

Mark the symmetry here, each part commencing with light.

Verse 16 would effectively cut at the root of those Eastern re-ligions in which the heavenly bodies are worshipped.

Verse 21 records the only distinct species mentioned in the chap-ter. It has been suggested that if these "sea monsters" refer to the crocodile, it is a quiet blow at prevalent Egyptian worship, which would be known to Moses. Notice the emphasis on God. He is mentioned thirty-two times with a variety of expressions: created (4), said (8), saw (8), made (7), called, set, divided, blessed. No other creation story has anything corresponding to verse 1. They all begin with an already existing creation or chaos (v. 2).

THE MESSAGE FOR MEDITATION

"In the beginning — God." As God was first in creation, so He is first in history, in providence, in redemption (Matt. 1:23) and ought, therefore, to be first in the individual life of each one of us.

Genesis 2

Verses 1-3 go with the preceding chapter, concluding the Creation Story. The Sabbath was the culminating point, expressive of rest after creation. Science shows that nothing is now being created. This is the first place where the word "sanctified" is found, and is the key to its meaning everywhere else, the root idea being separation or consecration.

Verse 4: "These are the generations." The first of eleven practically identical headings, which always point forward, never backward. In this verse it is expressive of the effects or results of the creation of the heaven and the earth. It is thus appropriately used in connection with the new name of God, which identifies Him with the God of chapter 1, and introduces Him as Jehovah, the Lord, as related to man. The word "day" summarizes what is found in the former chapter.

Verses 5-25 set out the character and circumstances of primitive man and prepare for the record of chapter 3.

Verses 4-7 show the nature of man to be twofold, related to earth and also to heaven. This is not another creation story, but another aspect, explaining the circumstances of man's life.

Verses 8-14: The environment of man's physical development. The locality of Eden is unknown, and the only geographical indications are found in the words Cush, Hiddekel (Tigris), Assyria, and Euphrates.

Verses 15-17: The opportunity for man's moral development. He was to work (v. 15), and he was also on probation (vv. 16, 17).

Verses 18-25: The need of man's social development. God saw it was not fitting or useful for him to be alone, and so a helper suitable for him, his "counterpart," was provided for the purpose of that fellowship which is of the essence of true life.

THE MESSAGE FOR MEDITATION

We have here the four vital and permanent principles of life: home, work, duty, and love. This shows what God intended for us, and the lines of our true development, if only sin had not entered the world.

Genesis 3

THIS CHAPTER is the pivot on which the whole Bible turns.

Verses 1-8: The choice of evil under temptation from outside. The serpent is one of the names found afterward for the Devil (2 Cor. 11:3; Rev. 12:9; 20:2). Three elements entered into temptation: physical desire, intellectual curiosity, and personal assertion. Two great truths are clear; (1) that God is not the author of sin; (2) that sin was due to an evil power outside man's own nature. Satan and the woman in their conversation used the term "God" and not "Lord God," because Jehovah is the covenant term, implying God's faithfulness. The consciousness of wrong immediately followed the act, and with this came shrinking from God, so different from their former life of fearless fellowship, which they had enjoyed before the Fall.

Verses 9-13: Conviction and confession. The sense of guilt was soon followed by a threefold sentence of condemnation. Subterfuges (v. 10) and attempts to blame others (vv. 12, 13) were powerless to avert the consequences.

Verses 14-19: Condemnation and promised redemption. First comes judgment on the serpent, the woman, and the man. Separation from Eden was inevitable, for sin and fellowship with God are always incompatible (Isa. 59:2). But with the condemnation came the announcement of an enmity which would lead to victory, and so we have here: (1) the curse, (2) the conflict, and (3) the conquest.

Verses 20, 21: Redemption is not only promised in word, but pictured in act. Man's attempt to cover his shame (v. 7) was useless, for no human covering could suffice. A beautiful symbol of the robe of righteousness.

Verses 22-24: God's providential care. It would have been disastrous if the man had, by eating of the tree of life, become immortal in his sinful state, and so, to prevent the catastrophe, God drove him from the garden.

THE MESSAGE FOR MEDITATION

Here and in Romans 8:33-35, sin and grace correspond. Adam and Eve were conscious of guilt, but in Christ we have no guilt (Rom. 8:33). They were also condemned, but in Christ there is no condemnation (v. 34). They were separated from Eden but in Christ, there is no separation (v. 35). Thus, where sin abounded, grace superabounds, and we rejoice in the glory of God's perfect redemption.

Genesis 4

FROM THE ORIGIN of sin to its progress. Sin in the individual develops in the family, and the conflict of good and evil (3:15) culminates in separation.

Verses 1-15: The first home. The parents, although expelled from Eden, are still influenced by the Divine promise, as the words of Eve at the birth of Cain show. The fact that the second son was named Abel ("vanity") perhaps suggests that the mother had already become disappointed in her hopes of her firstborn. The two brothers worshipped together, but while one offering was accepted, the other was not; and the explanation of the difference is that Abel offered "by faith" (Heb. 11:4), which pre-supposes a Divine revelation to which it is the response. Perhaps the coats of skins (3:21) are a hint of God's revelation of sacrifice through death as the way of approach to Him. Cain's anger shows that his worship was only a form of godliness without the power.

Verse 7 is difficult. It may mean: "If thou offerest not well, even then there is a sin-offering ready at hand for use as a propitiation. And not only so, but Abel thy brother will submit himself to thee as the first-born, and thou shalt exercise thy right of authority over him." Another rendering is: "If thou doest well, will there not be acceptance for thee? And if thou doest not well, sin is lying at the door, like a crouching beast ready to spring upon thee, and unto thee is sin's desire, but thou shouldst rule over it." The warning went unheeded, and murder was the result. Soon came the divine inquiry, condemnation, and judgment.

Verses 16-24: The two lines. Life develops first in the family, and then extends to society. Irreligion is seen in the line of

Cain. The progress is marked by the building of a city, a settled abode, polygamy, the beginnings of agriculture (v. 20), music (v. 21), and manufacture (v. 22). This development of an earthly civilization in connection with Cain's line is very significant.

Verses 25, 26: By contrast comes the line of Seth. The birth of Eve's third son raises her hopes once more, and in calling him Seth ("appointed"), she recognizes the divine providence. It would also seem, if the rendering is correct, that in connection with the son of Seth, there was a revival of true religion, the covenant name of Jehovah being mentioned, expressive of the promise made of victory over sin. Others interpret it to mean the opposite, a profanation of the Lord.

THE MESSAGE FOR MEDITATION

In this chapter we see the human developments, personal and social. Cain and Abel, represent two worshippers and two methods, and they mark the great fundamental principle of separation, which is found throughout Scripture. "Be ye separate."

Genesis 5

THIS CHAPTER GIVES the contrast of God's line through Seth with that of Satan through Cain (chap. 4).

Verse 1: The heading again is in 2:4.

Verse 3: The two likenesses, God's (v. 1) and Adam's.

Verses 3-32: Genealogy of Adam through Seth to Noah. The monotony is impressive and depressing — "and he died." It is only broken in Enoch (vv. 22-24) and Noah (vv. 28-32). The longevity is physiologically quite possible. Geology shows that conditions have been materially modified through the Flood. Fossils of elephants and other animals of the tropics found near the North Pole prove that, prior to the Flood, the climate of all the earth was genial and balmy. The chronology is probably not complete, as there are ten generations before the Flood and ten afterward, indicating a summary only. The Jews often shortened their genealogies (see Matt. 1), so long as the connection was clearly maintained. The antiquity of the world and of the human race is not a Biblical problem, and no computation is found based on any figures prior to the time of Abraham. The vital question is not the age but the *unity* of the race, the latter being the basis of all Bible doctrine (Rom. 5:12-21).

Verses 22-24: Enoch is one of the only two men who are recorded as having "walked with God" (6:9). Note his courageous testimony, in Jude 14, 15.

Verses 28-32 show Lamech's faith and hope.

THE MESSAGE FOR MEDITATION

(1) Enoch stands for fellowship with God, our highest privilege. (2) Noah suggests "rest" and "comfort," the two vital blessings of our life (Matt. 11:28-30).

Genesis 6

A RECORD OF antediluvian wickedness and its consequences, connected with and an outcome of chapter 4.

Verses 1-8: Some think "sons of God" means angels, as in Job 1:6 and Daniel 3:25, and that verse 2 refers to the angelic sin alluded to in Jude 6 and 2 Peter 2:4-6. But the simpler view is that the "sons of God" were the line of Seth, God's children (as in Deut. 14:1; Hosea 1:10; 11:1), and the "daughters of men" were Cain's line. The subsequent teaching of Scripture is clear against all intermarriage between Israelites and Canaanites.

Verse 2 accounts for the sin which led to the Flood, and verse 3 declares God's sentence upon man alone, and not on the angels for the sin recorded in verse 2. The "giants" are not said to be due to the facts in verse 2, but to have existed previously and subsequently.

Verse 3: The word "strive" means "dwell," and the message is one of warning that God's mercy was limited. Perhaps the 120 years mean the time yet to be given before the Flood, and certainly not the longevity of man.

Verse 5: Contrast God's sight here and in 1:31.

Verses 6, 7: God's attitude to sin expressed in the highest language we have, that of human life.

Verses 8-10: The contrast. The first mention of "grace," meaning God's favor and blessing, attitude and action.

Verses 11-13: Condition of the world and divine condemnation and decision.

Verses 14-16: God's command as to the ark. The cubit was about eighteen inches. The proportions agree with those of modern large vessels.

Verses 17-21: God's announcement of the Flood and His promise to Noah.

Verse 19 is the general command given long before the Flood; (7:2) the special one when the time had come.

THE MESSAGE FOR MEDITATION

Contrast (1) the days of Noah (Matt. 24:37-39), and (2) the faith of Noah (6:22; Heb. 11:7). Sin and safety. Although we may live surrounded by evil, God's grace through Christ can keep us from harm.

Genesis 7

THE DETAILS of the Flood after the brief summary of chapters 1-5 are very significant, showing the religious purpose of Genesis.

Verse 1: The divine invitation and testimony. First occasion of the word "righteous" (see 15:6).

Verses 2-4: The divine instructions given just before the Flood. For the distinction between clean and unclean, see Leviticus 1:2, 10, 14; 11:3; 13:31; Genesis 15:9.

Verses 5-9: Noah's obedience, prompt, full (v. 5), and unquestioning.

Verses 10-24: The Flood. Forty days of rain (v. 12), and one hundred and fifty of inundation (v. 24). Note (1) the preservation of the godly (vv. 13-16); (2) the condemnation of the ungodly (vv. 17-23). The evidence for a Flood is very strong, quite apart from Genesis. The story is a unity, and if each mark of time is noted, from 7:6 onwards, the duration of the Flood will be seen to harmonize with all the statements made. The account is natural, historical, simple, with nothing mythical or unworthy. It is written from the standpoint of an eye-witness. There is a universal tradition as to a Flood, and geology affords clear indications of such a catastrophe. The use of the Divine Name is very striking. God (*Elohim*) is the God of judgment. Lord (*Jehovah*) is the God of grace. Each instance is impressive and significant. See both in verse 16, where judgment commands and grace keeps.

THE MESSAGE FOR MEDITATION

(1) The spiritual position (v. 1) — "righteous before me." Noah was "right with God." This is for us *in* Christ. (2) The practical proof (vv. 5, 9) — "did according to all." Obedience is the best testimony to righteousness. This is for us *through* Christ.

Genesis 8

THE CLOSING DAYS of the Flood and the commencement of the new era.

Verses 1-5: God's action. The judgment drew to an end. God was mindful of His servant.

Verses 6-14: Noah's attitude. His faith (vv. 6, 7); his hope (vv. 8, 9); his patience (vv. 10-14).

Verses 15-17: God's command.

Verses 18-20: Noah's consecration. Obedience was followed by worship. First mention of "altar" and "burnt-offerings." The spiritual thought of the latter was consecration, not expiation (Rom. 12:1). Noah thus showed his readiness to put God first in his life.

Verses 21, 22: God's revelation. First came the divine acceptance (v. 21), and then the divine assurance (vv. 21, 22). The language used is suited to the spiritual comprehension of man, and signifies God's endorsement of His servant's attitude. The divine testimony to man's sinfulness is clear, and is given as a reason for the avoidance of another judgment on the earth. The assurance of the constant and permanent recurrence of the seasons is promised in an eightfold alternation. Judgment gives way to mercy, and grace is seen in the very laws of nature.

THE MESSAGE FOR MEDITATION

God's relation to His servant is threefold: Thought (v. 1); Command (v. 15); Promise (vv. 21, 22). This is the continual attitude of God to His children. He is mindful of us, He tells us what to do, and He assures us of blessing.

Genesis 9

A FRESH START. Noah becomes the second head of the race. *Verses* 1-7: The New Commencement. It springs from the divine blessing (v. 1). Then comes the exhortation (v. 1), the assurance (v. 2), the provision (v. 3), the prohibition (v 4), the warning (vv. 5, 6), and the renewed exhortation (v. 7). These verses should be compared with the original revelation to Adam (1:24-28).

Verses 8-17: The New Covenant. Grace is always provided to meet needs, and this covenant was the assurance that what God required (vv. 1-7) He would provide. The various features of the covenant are noteworthy. (1) Its Source — God. Note the emphasis in verses 9, 11, 12, 15, 17. (2) Its Scope — with the lower creation as well (vv. 9, 10). (3) Its Purpose — guarantee of safety (v. 11). (4) Its Pledge — the rainbow, a natural phenomenon, now used as a visible sign (vv. 12, 13). (5) Its Meaning — God's faithfulness in spite of appearances to the contrary (vv. 14, 15). (6) Its Duration — everlasting (v. 16). (7) Its Guarantee — God's Word (v. 17).

Verses 18, 19: Noah's sons named here again (5:32; 6:10; 7:13), because the narrative is now specially concerned with them. "Canaan" anticipates 10:6, to prepare for v. 25. These three are the heads of the race, and science today tells of the great sources of all mankind.

Verses 20, 21: The two sins, drunkenness and immodesty, are often associated. This is the first record of both. Noah sinned in the course of his ordinary life. Legitimate occupations may be the occasions of evil.

Verses 22, 23: Shame and sorrow. Contrast the actions of the three brothers. The sin against filial love and the devotion of loving loyalty.

Verses 24-27: Retribution and reward. It is difficult to understand the inclusion of Canaan and the omission of Ham. Perhaps the son was associated with his father's sin. Note the curse (the third; 3:14-17; 4:11). The servitude of Canaan was seen in later times. Shem was blessed and Japheth was to be enlarged. The latter stands for the Gentile nations.

Verses 28, 29: The summary of Noah's subsequent life. Though the sin was never repeated, the memory must have cast a cloud to the end.

THE MESSAGE FOR MEDITATION

God's Covenant of Grace: Its Promise; Its Provision; Its Pledge; Its Power. There was no need for Noah to sin if only

he had remembered and rested on God's protection. Let us rest
and rejoice in God's abundant and unchangeable grace. "He
is able," and therefore "we are well able."

Genesis 10

A REMARKABLE illustration of the purpose of Genesis. After
chapter 5, Adam to Noah, we have here the further connection
of Noah with Terah the father of Abraham.

In verse 1 the usual order appears of Shem, Ham, and Japheth,
but in the chapter the opposite is seen, because Genesis always
deals with collateral branches first, and then with the main line of
Shem. These nations are seen to be akin to the chosen race from
which God's blessings were to spring (12:1-3).

Note the fourfold development mentioned in verses 5, 20, 32,
expressive of the varied classification into individual, tribal, and
national aspects.

Verses 2-5: The family of Japheth. He was the oldest son
(v. 21). Fourteen nations are associated with him.

Verses 6-20: The family of Ham. Thirty nations are mentioned.
Nimrod is specially mentioned as indicative of opposition to
God, as seen in Babel (11:1-9). Canaan is prominent (vv. 15-19)
because of the subsequent history in relation to Israel.

Verses 21-31: The family of Shem. Twenty-six nations are
found here. Shem was the youngest son. "Eber" suggests
"Hebrew," and in his son's time occurred the confusion of Babel
(v. 25). These nations total seventy, as in 46:27 and Exodus
24:1-9. The authenticity of this chapter is seen from the fact
that, as late as 1 Chronicles, chapter 1, nothing more was known.
Ethnology agrees with this record in dividing mankind into three
primary groups.

THE MESSAGE FOR MEDITATION

All men have (1) oneness of origin; (2) oneness of need
(through sin); (3) oneness of redemption (through Shem).
This is at once humbling and inspiring. "I'm a poor sinner, and
nothing at all, but Jesus Christ is my all in all."

Genesis 11

ANOTHER REMARKABLE contrast of human sin and divine purpose.

Verses 1-9: The story of Babel. The fertility of Shinar naturally led to the thought of permanent stay and close association, but these innocent desires degenerated into evil, and pride and ambition were the outcome (v. 4). But this sin could not but provoke divine judgment. Confusion of language led to dispersion, and thus to the failure of the project. Philology supports this record in regard to the division of languages. The judgment of the chapter is seen to be overruled in the glorious unity of language in Acts 2, and its culmination in Revelation 7:9.

Verses 10-26: A fresh movement. The race as a whole is now dismissed, and attention concentrated on one line and one man. Everything hitherto has been preparing for this. The genealogy of Abraham from Shem.

Verses 27, 28: Birth of Abram from Terah. Abram was almost certainly the youngest son.

Verses 29, 30: Marriage of Abram to Sarai.

Verses 31, 32: The first call of Abram. A third start with humanity. The first call came at Ur (Acts 7:2-4), and Terah apparently was influenced to go also. Idolatry had been rife in Abram's family (Josh. 24:2, 15; Isa. 51: 1, 2). Why did Abram stay in Haran? Was it an undue partiality for his father?

THE MESSAGE FOR MEDITATION

(1) Wilfulness at Babel. (2) Willingness in Abram. What a contrast! Man's sin in going contrary to God, and a man's readiness to do the will of God.

Genesis 12

THE LIFE OF ABRAHAM covers over thirteen chapters, thereby showing its importance.

Verses 1-3: The Divine Call. The second call in Haran (Acts 7:2-4). The great principle was Separation. The threefold promise: land, seed, universal blessing.

Verses 4-9: The Human Response. Mark the features: Confidence (based on God's word, v. 4); Obedience (vv. 4-6); Influence (Lot led to accompany him, v. 5); Confession (altar, vv. 6, 7);

Endurance (waited, vv. 8, 9). In verse 7 is recorded the first visible appearance of God. Hitherto the revelations had been by voice only.

Verse 10: The famine was a test of faith, coming soon after a season of communion. The journey was "natural," but Abraham should have trusted God still further. This would have been "supernatural." The easy way is not always the right way.

Verses 11-13: The proposal. Moral weakness coming after moral strength. The suggestion was a "half-truth" (20:12). Verbally true, but actually false. It was also selfish, with no thought for Sarai.

Verses 14-20: The results. (1) To Sarai, danger (vv. 14-16); (2) To Pharaoh, Divine displeasure (v. 17); (3) To Abraham, rebuke (vv. 18-20). A child of God rebuked by a man of the world.

THE MESSAGE FOR MEDITATION

(1) Splendid faith (vv. 1-9; (2) Sad failure (vv. 10-20). The only safeguards are *truth* and *trust*.

Genesis 13

Verses 1-4: Restoration. Abraham returned to Canaan, and set up tent and altar (home and church), where he formerly lived. Note phrases "at the beginning" and "at the first." No altar in Egypt, because Abraham was then out of communion. Now the believer is restored to fellowship.

Verses 5, 6: The Problem. Uncle and nephew were both wealthy. First instance of riches in Scripture (v. 2). No sin in possessing wealth if we regard ourselves as only stewards, not owners. We may have riches if only riches do not have *us*.

Verse 7: The Strife. With the Canaanites looking on, it was very sad that any difference should arise between two of God's children.

Verses 8, 9: The Proposal. Abraham with rare magnanimity, although the older man, took the initiative in suggesting a separation. "The servant of God must not strive" (2 Tim. 2:24).

Verses 10-13: The Choice. Lot, the younger, selfishly chose the best district, one by which his possessions might still further increase. But the choice was full of danger, because the land was in the direction of Sodom, and to be near was only one step from being within.

Verses 14-17: The Compensation. God would not allow His servant to suffer. The promise was even fuller than in 12:1, 7.

Verse 18: The Response. Again Abraham acknowledged God by erecting tent and altar, the places of home and worship.

THE MESSAGE FOR MEDITATION

A contrast between believers: (1) Compromise; (2) Consecration.

Genesis 14

A NEW EMERGENCY for a believer, and his ability to meet it.

Verses 1-11: The Battle. Clearly this is a contemporary record. Elam was supreme, and felt it necessary to keep the Jordan valley free, because of the trade-route to Egypt. Research has now fully demonstrated the historical character of the story.

Verse 12: Lot was captured because from near Sodom (13:12), he had entered into it (14:12). The consequences of selfishness and compromise are disastrous.

Verses 13-16: When Abraham heard, he at once magnanimously took action. A new situation calling for the exercise of new powers. The bold pursuit of 120 miles ended in a splendid success. Prompt action, skilful leadership, and great courage were combined in this man of God.

Verses 17, 18: Success is a good test of character. Gratitude prompted the king of Sodom to recognize Abraham's services. The other king acted very differently.

Verses 18-20: He was one of the line of Shem that still worshipped the true God. His idea of God was that of the Supreme Being. As priest he represented man to God (Heb. 5:1), and as king he blessed Abraham.

Verse 20: Abraham at once recognized the greatness and superiority of Melchizedek by receiving blessing and giving tithes.

Verse 21: The Proposal. This was natural and customary, a dividing of the spoils.

Verses 22-24: The Refusal. His relation to God prevented this. The exception made was in reference to those who had not his spiritual insight.

THE MESSAGE FOR MEDITATION
(1) Faith seen in new circumstances. (2) Faith seen in clear insight. (3) Faith shown in splendid courage.

Genesis 15

THE DIVINE ENCOURAGEMENT.

Verse 1: The Revelation. Times of spiritual reaction often come (I Kings 19 after 18). So with Abraham now; and God met him just when he needed the cheer. This is the fifth of God's nine manifestations to Abraham. Perhaps Abraham had some fear after the victory, and so God cheered him. "Fear not" and "Be not afraid" occur about 84 times in Scripture. God would be his shield (Psa. 3:3; 91:4), and his reward, in spite of, and because of, his refusal of the spoil.

Verses 2, 3: The Response. Abraham is despondent and disappointed.

Verses 4, 5: The Assurance. God dealt lovingly, correcting his faithlessness and instructing and encouraging his faith.

Verse 6: The Acceptance. The divine word caused an immediate and wonderful change. He took God at His word. Faith is our response to God's revelation. Then God responded, and regarded His servant as righteous. This means the state of being "right" with God, and is found here for the first time. Note here the first occasion of five words and phrases: "the word of the Lord came;" "fear not;" "believed;" "counted;" "righteous."

Verse 7: The Fresh Assurance. In response to Abraham's faith, God entered into covenant. The basis is God's character.

Verse 8: The Natural Inquiry. Abraham wanted knowledge, certitude, proof. Not because of faithlessness, but for confirmation.

Verses 9-21: The Great Covenant. The usual method was adopted (Lev. 1:6; Jer. 34:18, 19). God's revelation was fourfold and then came the symbolical action (v. 17) and assurance (vv. 18-21).

THE MESSAGE FOR MEDITATION

Covenants in Scripture are marked by (1) divine promise and action. (2) Human belief and acceptance. God alone passed through the pieces, Abraham being asleep. God's covenants are not mutual agreements on equal terms, but divine bestowals in which God does everything and man only receives and enjoys (Heb. 6:17; Psa. 116:12, 13).

Genesis 16

THE COVENANT DOUBTED — A false step.

Verses 1-3: The Mistake.   After the experience recorded in chapter 15, Abraham might have been expected to proceed safely and happily along the pathway of God's will.   But a new temptation came through his wife, and he fell.   Perhaps Sarai was impatient, as she had not been clearly told she was to be the mother of the promised seed.   Her motive was good, and marked by faith in God's promise, but her action, though customary and legal in those days, was wrong.   She should have awaited God's time and way.

Verses 4-6: The results were pride (v. 4), jealousy (v. 5), misery (v. 6), and injustice (v. 6).   They were inevitable.

Verses 7-12: The Interposition.   Man blunders, but God intervenes.   There was His interest in human troubles (v. 7), His call for perfect submission (vv. 8, 9), His assurance of definite blessing (v. 10), and His revelation of overruling providence (vv. 11, 12).   Hagar quickly responded, realizing the divine presence (v. 13), making a memorial of God's promise (v. 14), and showing obedience to His will.

THE MESSAGE FOR MEDITATION

(1) Special peril often comes after special privilege.   (2) Strong temptation may arise (chap. 15) from surprising sources. (3) Simple faith should be united with sincere patience (Heb. 6:12).

Genesis 17

GOD'S TIME for blessing came at length.

Verses 1-8: The New Revelation.   Ten years since the trouble with Hagar (16:16).   Now a fresh appearance of God and a fresh message (v. 1).   The new title means "The mighty God" or "The sufficient God."   New responsibilities are named (v. 1).   The result is soon seen in reverence.   Then comes fellowship (v. 3) and strong assurance (v. 4).   The new revelation is threefold; Abraham, the land, and the seed.

Verses 9-14: The Requirements. Abraham is to obey in order to enjoy. Circumcision, an Eastern custom, meant separation and purity. Here we see God's covenant with young life. He is their Father.

Verses 15, 16: The Further Revelation. Now a definite message is given about Sarah.

Verses 17, 18: The Response. Abraham is astonished but trustful: it is the laugh of faith, not of unbelief. But there is one great difficulty, Ishmael, and the appeal is very touching.

Verses 19-22: The Full Revelation. But God's will must be done, though Ishmael shall not be forgotten. God would overrule.

Verses 23-27: The Reception. Abraham's obedience was prompt (v. 23) and full (v. 27).

THE MESSAGE FOR MEDITATION

New views of God: (1) His character (v. 1); (2) His will; (3) His purpose; (4) His love.

Genesis 18

THE SUPREME characteristic of a believer's life is fellowship with God.

Verses 1-8: The Appearance. God came as a Guest. The three men were a manifestation of God in visible form, together with two created angels. Abraham's response was marked by true Eastern politeness and hospitality. Hospitality is a prominent feature of the Christian life (Rom. 12:13; 1 Tim. 3:2; Heb. 13:2).

Verses 9-15: The Assurance. The inquiry about Sarah, and the renewal of the promise were followed by Sarah's incredulity. This is one of several indications that her spiritual life was not very closely akin to Abraham's. But she was rebuked and taught.

Verses 16-21: The Announcement. A further revelation was now given. God's confidence in Abraham (v. 16), the revelation of His purpose and its reasons.

Verses 18, 19 are followed by the disclosure of the divine judgment on Sodom and Gomorrah.

Verses 22-33: The Appeal. Abraham is the only one in the Old Testament called the Friend of God (2 Chron. 20:7; Isa. 41:8; James 2:23), and this chapter is the special proof of this fellowship, with its characteristic of intercession. (1) Abraham's position was one of great privilege (vv. 22, 23). (2) His spirit was earnest (vv. 23, 24). (3) His plea was urgent (vv. 23, 25). (4) His prayer was encouraged (v. 26). (5) His humility was profound (v. 27). (6) His persistence was great (vv. 29-32). (7) His silence was significant (v. 33). Abraham ceased asking before God ceased promising.

THE MESSAGE FOR MEDITATION

(1) Fellowship in knowledge (vv. 1-21; John 15:15). (2) Fellowship in intercession (vv. 22-33; John 15:7).

Genesis 19

LOT IS ONE of the beacons of the Bible.

Verses 1-3: The Visit of the Angels. It is curious that Lot should have returned to Sodom after the rescue (chap. 14). The two created angels went to Sodom, while the divine Personage remained with Abraham. Lot's invitation was met with a strange refusal, perhaps because they were there for exploration and judgment.

Verses 4-11: The Depravity of the Place. The sin is unmentionable, though it is perpetuated by a certain word derived from this chapter. Lot's readiness to sacrifice his daughters so as to save himself is the depth of selfishness.

Verses 12-14: The Warning of the Angels. Their errand is stated in the plainest terms. Lot's appeal fell on deaf ears. It had no power over the men of Sodom because he had been one of them too long. Life and lips did not correspond.

Verses 15-22: The Urgency of the Deliverance. The lingering of Lot and the patience of God are very striking. And then are seen in contrast the weakness of Lot and the mercy of God.

Verses 23-26: The Judgment of God. Lot's wife, like himself, was attracted to Sodom, and looking back was engulfed by the lava. With father and mother so weak, it is not surprising to see the results in the family.

Verses 27-29: The Mercy of God. Abraham's intercession had prevailed, and on account of it Lot was delivered. God heard His servant for four only (18: 32).

Verses 30-38: The Depths of Degradation. It is both impossible and unnecessary to comment. The terrible results in Moab's and Ammon's enmity to Israel were seen in future days. Lot disappears into unutterable shame and inevitable oblivion.

THE MESSAGE FOR MEDITATION

(1) The Sins of Sodom, calling for divine judgment. (2) The Sins of Lot, calling for divine discipline — "Saved, yet so as by fire."

Genesis 20

AN OLD SIN REPEATED. The evil nature remains in the believer.

Verses 1, 2: The Sin. Abraham journeyed toward the southern district, perhaps for pasturage, or to be free from the surroundings described in chap. 19. As before (12:13), Abraham said Sarah was his sister. Abraham thus feared man, showed selfishness, told a lie, and distrusted God. At once, Abimelech took steps, doubtless in honor, to make her his wife, thinking that alliance with a powerful man like Abraham would be advantageous. This repetition of the sin is unfortunately true to human nature.

Verses 3-8: The Interposition. God saved His servant from himself. In view of the promised seed, Sarah was protected. But what a sad thing to see, the character of an unbeliever shining out in a superior way to that of a believer.

Verses 9-16: The Rebuke. A child of God rebuked by a man of the world. Abraham tried to justify his conduct (vv. 11-13), but this was really a condemnation. Abimelech's gifts to Abraham and Sarah were a sort of acknowledgment and propitiation, and "thy brother" (v. 16) reads almost sarcastically. Abimelech is at his best, Abraham at his worst.

Verses 17, 18: The Outcome. God overruled all these mistakes. If He had not interposed, how terrible would have been the effects of this sin!

THE MESSAGE FOR MEDITATION

(1) Sin in believers is a fact, a force and a peril. (2) Sin in believers need not be a cause of trouble (Rom. 8:2; Gal. 5:16, A.S.V.; Gal. 5:25).

Genesis 21

NEW LESSONS are always being taught to the believer.

Verses 1-8: The Fulfillment. At length God's word was accomplished. Romans 4:19 illustrates the faith of Abraham. The naming and the circumcision prove this faith, and Sarah's laugh is no longer that of incredulity (18:13). The weaning in Eastern fashion would be when Isaac was three to five years old (Psa. 131:2; Isa. 28:9; Matt. 21:16).

Verses 9-11: The Sadness. The result of Abraham's mistake and sin now show themselves. Ishmael was seventeen and his disappointment would be great. The mockery is called persecution in Galatians 4:29. Sarah resented this and acted accordingly.

Verses 12-14: The Overruling. God's interposition alone could straighten out this tangled skein. He comforted Abraham (v. 12), guided him wisely (v. 12), and encouraged him (v. 13). With true faith Abraham responded (v. 14).

Verses 15-21: The Proof. The test for Hagar soon came, but God was true to His word, and not only saved Ishmael from death, but blessed and prospered his future.

Verses 22-34: The Daily Round. Abraham is seen here in ordinary life, and shows features of his character. The testimony of the Canaanite king and his captain is significant (v. 22), and the request impressive (v. 23). Abimelech evidently realized Abraham's power and importance. The patriarch quickly responded, though he felt it necessary to remonstrate. But an explanation was soon forthcoming, and a covenant was thereupon made. Then came a new testimony to God (v. 33), and a new revelation of God in the new name, telling of God's unchangeableness. This was an advance on 14:22 and 17:1.

THE MESSAGE FOR MEDITATION

(1) Sunshine (vv. 1-8). (2) Shadows (vv. 9-21). (3) Sunshine again (vv. 22-34). "God is faithful."

Genesis 22

THE SUPREME crisis in Abraham's life.

Verses 1, 2: The Test. The time is noteworthy. It was just after the new revelation of God (21:33, 34), which prepared him for it. "Tempt" means "test" or "prove" (James 1:12-15). The fourfold description of Isaac is striking. Moriah was one of the mountains in which Jerusalem was situated (2 Chron. 3:1).

Verses 3-10: The Trial. Abraham's alacrity is wonderful, showing his faith (Psa. 119:60; Gal. 1:16). He evidently expected to return with Isaac (v. 5). The conversation between father and son is beautiful, indicating real faith in both of them.

Verses 11-14: The Triumph. God's interposition was at the right moment (Psa. 107:27, 28), and Abraham's faith had been fully proved. This faith was confirmed by the provision of the ram — "The Lord will see to it" (Rom. 5:10).

Verses 15-19: The Testimony. The divine voice recognized what had been done, and renewed the promise with an oath (Heb. 6:13, 14). And then Abraham and his son returned to the young men. Abraham evidently had felt sure that God would at once raise Isaac from the dead (Heb. 11:17-19), and this faith was the more remarkable because there had not been a resurrection before.

Verses 20-24: The Tidings. News came to Abraham from afar, and the family line is given.

THE MESSAGE FOR MEDITATION

Aspects of Faith. (1) Its character — taking God at His word. (2) Its thoroughness — not a question. (3) Its secret — knowing God and having fellowship with Him. (4) Its vindication — God's testimony to His servant.

Genesis 23

AFTER CHAPTER 22, Abraham lived an almost entirely uneventful life for twenty-five years.

Verses 1, 2: Death. The removal of Abraham's lifelong companion, not quite of his own spiritual stature, but evidently for sixty years his true and loyal wife.

Verse 2: Sorrow. The first record of a man's tears.

Verse 3: Duty. The great safeguard against overmuch sorrow is work.

Verses 4-18: Faith. The dialogue is remarkable. Abraham's testimony (v. 4), his courtesy (v. 7), his persistence (vv. 8, 9), and the arrangement made, are noteworthy. Although God had promised him the land, he would not be unjust to the existing owners.

Verses 19, 20: Love. The first grave recorded in Scripture. Abraham had done all he could for his beloved wife.

The Message for Meditation

A picture of home-life in time of sorrow. (1) Love. (2) Service. (3) Hope. Blessed are the homes where these elements are seen.

Genesis 24

The closing scenes of a noble life.

Verses 1-9: God's present blessings (v. 1) did not make Abraham forget the future (vv. 2, 4) and the promise of God. The conversation shows his insight (vv. 6, 7) and his assurance of God's blessing (vv. 7-9).

Verses 10-14: The obedience and zealous interest of the servant are significant. The man was in full spiritual sympathy with his master.

Verses 15-33: With courtesy (v. 17), patience (v. 21), and wisdom (v. 22) he proceeds with his task, and recognizes God's hand in everything (vv. 26, 27).

Verses 34-49: Faithfully and wisely he carries through his commission. The conversation is deeply interesting. After stating his position (v. 34) and praising his master (vv. 35, 36), he declares his errand (vv. 37-48), and makes the proposal (v. 49).

Verses 50-67: Success crowns his efforts and soon the purpose is accomplished and Rebecca goes with him.

The Message for Meditation

Notice the spiritual suggestions underlying the narrative. (1) The father seeking a bride for the son (Matt. 22:2). (2) The son as the father's one thought (Eph. 1:20-22). (3) The servant's part. (4) The attractive power of the message (John 12:32). (5) The response to the message — "I will go." (6) The glorious position of the bride (Eph. 1:4).

Genesis 25

Verses 1-6: Abraham's second marriage. He evidently showed that his closing years were marked by fresh vigor of body and mind. One of the sons was Midian, whose descendants became bitter enemies of Israel. But Isaac's position was made clear and safe (v. 5).

Verses 7-10: A beautiful description of Abraham's death (v. 8), showing faith in a future life, for the words cannot refer to his grave (35:29; 49:33). The two sons meet at the funeral. Death is a great healer of breaches. Reviewing Abraham's life, we notice particularly his (1) faith, (2) faithfulness (Gal. 3:9), (3) reverence for God, and (4) the reality of his fellowship.

Verse 11: The death of Abraham made no difference to the faithfulness of God to His promises.

Verses 12-18: The generations of Ishmael. The collateral branch is again put first and then dismissed. The record here is brief, in accordance with the main purpose of Genesis.

Verse 19: The opening of another chapter in the history of the unfolding of God's plans.

Verse 20 summarizes chapter 24. The section dealing with the generations of Isaac extends to 35:29.

Verses 20-23: After twenty years (v. 26), there was no fulfillment of God's promise. But in this test of faith, Isaac did the best thing possible, he spoke to God about it. The answer soon came. God's delays are not necessarily refusals. Then followed perplexity to Rebecca, and she, too, took her difficulty to God, whose explanation was both clear and startling, indicating His sovereignty. The younger son is again chosen for God's will, which, though not understood by us, is supreme (Eph. 1:5, 9, 11).

Verses 24-28: Unlike from the first, the two sons developed on distinct lines, and the parental affection also showed this fundamental difference.

Verses 29-34: God's will about the future (v. 23) was evidently known to Esau and Jacob. Esau set little store by the birthright. Jacob valued it, and knowing his brother's weakness took advantage of it, and obtained the coveted privilege under a solemn oath. Esau, with all his outward attractiveness, was a purely secular man. Jacob, with all his outward unattractiveness, was definitely impressed with the reality of the heritage promised to Abraham and Isaac.

THE MESSAGE FOR MEDITATION

(1) Let us learn the value of prayer to God in perplexities (vv. 21-23). (2) Let us note the necessity of waiting for God's time and way in emergencies (vv. 30-34). The secret of all our

life lies in seeking to know and then learning to do the will of God.

Genesis 26

ALTHOUGH ISAAC lived longer than the other patriarchs, much less is recorded of him. This is the only chapter exclusively devoted to him.

Verses 1-5: Difficulty met by divine guidance. Prohibited from going into Egypt, the promises to Abraham were repeated and confirmed. Comparison with other passages shows some new feature each time.

Verses 6-11: Difficulty met by human sin. Following his father's example, and actuated by fear and selfishness, he told a lie. It was sadly natural for him to do what Abraham had done, because of the probable advantages. Again, the believer is rebuked by the outsider. There is nothing sadder than this.

Verses 12-17: Difficulty met by divine blessing. He was publicly blessed even though he had been privately unfaithful. God sometimes shields His children from outside harm even when He has to deal with them severely in private (Num. 14:22; 23:21). But jealousy soon showed itself.

Verses 18-22: Difficulty met by human patience. Why Isaac should have remained in Philistia is puzzling, unless it was due to lack of faith in the power of God. This reluctance to go far away led to trouble, for the Philistines were evidently trying to make things uncomfortable, and compel Isaac to return home. But the spirit of yielding prevailed (v. 22), and Isaac saw in it a mark of God's blessing.

Verses 23-33: Difficulty met by divine favor. At length, Isaac returned home and it is striking to note the immediate result (v. 24, "the same night"). God never meant him to go even to Gerar, but at last he is in the line of the divine will. This is the first record of the title "the God of Abraham." Obedience is always the pathway of revelation and blessing (Psa. 25:9). Isaac's response was immediate, and thorough, and the results were unmistakable. (1) The altar meant consecration. (2) The prayer expressed need. (3) The tent suggested home. (4) The well indicated provision. And then came testimony from outside. Those who were formerly hostile became friends.

Verses 34, 35: A further proof of Esau's lack of spiritual affinity with Isaac and Rebecca.

THE MESSAGE FOR MEDITATION

(1) God should be put and kept first in our life. (2) Truth should always actuate and dominate our way. (3) Separation from the world should ever mark our attitude. And for all this God provides adequate and abundant grace (2 Cor. 9:8).

Genesis 27

AN UNPLEASANT PICTURE of family life, all the members being involved in wrongdoing.

Verses 1-4: The father's plot. Isaac was not near death, for he lived forty years more. He knew God's will (25:23) and yet tried to thwart it because of favoritism for Esau. Esau also knew, but was ready to fall in with his father's project.

Verses 5-17: The mother's counter-plot. Her aim was good but her methods wrong. Jacob saw the risk (v. 12), but was overborne by his mother.

Verses 18-29: The younger son's deception. The lies were terrible but the father's benediction naturally followed.

Verses 30-40: The elder son's defeat. Sympathy with Esau cannot hide the fact that he had come to realize the true nature of the blessing. But it was too late, and he could not change his father's mind (this is the true view of Hebrews 12:17), could not undo what he had done.

Verses 41-46: The outcome. Esau's anger was natural, but as Isaac did not die he could not vent it on Jacob. Meanwhile, Rebecca promptly took action to thwart it, but with all her resourcefulness she could not foresee either that she might never meet Jacob again, or that her brother, Laban, would prove as great a plotter as was she.

THE MESSAGE FOR MEDITATION

Some very solemn and searching lessons for us all. (1) The end does *not* justify the means. (2) The results of sin are inevitable (all four suffered irreparably). (3) The will of God will be done in spite of man's efforts to thwart it (Psa. 33:10; Prov. 16:9; 19:21).

Genesis 28

Verses 1-5: Rebecca's suggestion is accepted by Isaac, who now realizes fully the will of God for Jacob. This is the last thing recorded of Isaac although he lived over forty years after this event. Does this mean that God set him aside as a comparative failure?

Verses 6-9: Esau's marriage was another attempt to regain the blessing, by trying to please his parents in Jacob's absence. But his choice showed he had no sense of spiritual realities. He does not do exactly what God requires but something like it. But at heart he was unchanged.

Verses 10-12: The lonely traveller was reminded by the ladder in his dream, first of the distance between his soul and God through his sin, and then of the way in which he could reach God.

Verses 13-15: The revelation of God was at once specific and inspiring, telling of (1) God's character, (2) the land, and (3) the seed. Then comes fourfold assurance of God's presence, protection, preservation and power.

Verses 16-22: The response was threefold. (1) A consciousness of God's presence (vv. 16, 17). (2) A memorial (vv. 18, 19). (3) A vow (vv. 20-22). Evidently he was deeply impressed. It was his first direct contact with God, and the vow (mentioned here for the first time) shows how deeply he felt his need of the divine presence and favor. This story of Bethel made its mark on subsequent generations (Hos. 12:4; John 1:51).

THE MESSAGE FOR MEDITATION

(1) The ladder symbolizes God's condescending grace, coming in Christ from heaven to earth. (2) The angels suggest God's free grace, as without hindrance they went up and down the ladder. (3) The divine words declare God's sufficient grace, for in that revelation was found all that Jacob needed.

Genesis 29

CHAPTERS 29 to 31 cover important years of Jacob's life, and show him in the school of experience.

Verse 1: The start. The Hebrew is, "Jacob lifted up his feet," suggesting new hope as he went on his journey of 450 miles.

Verses 2-14: The meeting. The providence of God is seen, and when Rachel comes it is easy to realize Jacob's attitude. Faith had come into his life at Bethel, and now came the love

of a woman, God's second best gift. The welcome from Laban
was genuine and hearty.

Verses 15-20: The service. Laban's agreement was fair, not
presuming on relationship to get the work done for nothing.
Jacob's service was inspired by his deep love. As Coleridge says,
"No man could be a bad man who loved as Jacob loved Rachel."

Verses 21-30: The disappointment. Then came the first experience of treachery. Jacob was now in a school of discipline,
and was being dealt with as he had treated his brother. His love
for Rachel was so strong, that he did not mind serving another
seven years for her after he had obtained her as his wife.

Verses 31-35: The further training. The possession of two
wives brought its inevitable trouble, but God was teaching Jacob
thereby.

THE MESSAGE FOR MEDITATION

(1) Jacob began to experience a severe discipline. Discipline
is often training of and for "discipleship." (2) But he also made
a striking discovery. He realized that God was just and was
repaying him with what he himself had done. Every believer
knows how true it is that we reap as we sow. Forgiveness blots
out sin, but consequences often remain to chasten and train.

Genesis 30

THE DISCIPLINE is prolonged and even heightened.

Verses 1, 2: It is clear that Rachel was never in full spiritual
sympathy with Jacob. Husband and wife were on different levels.

Verses 3-8: A deplorable action, due to Rachel, though one
that, according to prevalent custom, she had absolute power to
require.

Verses 9-13: A similar action by Leah, and equally unfor-
tunate.

Verses 14-24: Some of the inevitable results of polygamy:
envy, jealousy, and household friction. Who can doubt the effect
of all this in the characters of the children? This is seen later on.

Verses 25-43: After twenty years (31:38, 44), Jacob's thoughts
turned toward his home, and the birth of Joseph seems to have
been a turning-point. But Laban did not want to lose so valuable
a worker, and an arrangement was made between them. Laban
then began to work for his own advantage and against Jacob

(vv. 34, 35), but Jacob was more than a match for him (vv. 37-43).

THE MESSAGE FOR MEDITATION

(1) A wonderful testimony (v. 27). God blessed the man of the world for the sake of His servant. (2) A deplorable testimony. Jacob's plot was unutterably sad after Bethel and was inexcusable. He could not and would not trust his God. We always degenerate if we do not honor God.

Genesis 31

THE CLIMAX of the stay at Haran.

Verses 1-3: The crisis. Jacob's prosperity caused envy and bitterness. Then God interposed.

Verses 4-16: The consultation. Jacob first tells his wives of their father's action, and of what he regarded as God's protection, though he says nothing of his own wrong-doing. To him the end always justified the means. The wives sided with Jacob against their father, whom they doubtless knew well, by experience.

Verses 17-21: The flight. With characteristic promptness Jacob set out. But trouble was at hand. Rachel had retained her Syrian superstition. It was always Rachel, not Leah, who caused Jacob trouble.

Verses 22-24: The pursuit. Laban's intentions were met by God's action. He had to reckon on One stronger than Jacob. Laban was the chief and first offender.

Verses 25-35: The expostulation. Laban's "air of injured innocence" is an illustration of his hypocrisy. His words of affection are either unreal or merely impulsive, for nothing like this has been seen in his acts for long years.

Verses 36-42: The vindication. Jacob then boldly spoke for himself, and showed Laban the real meaning of God's intervention.

Verses 43-55: The covenant. Then the two men made an agreement, using names that implied that neither trusted the other, and that God must be the safeguard for both when they were out of each other's sight.

THE MESSAGE FOR MEDITATION

We see here how God should be real to us in daily life. (1) God's will shown. Mark the steps: desire (30:25); circumstances (31:2); command (31:3). (2) God's way followed. All four — Laban, Jacob, Rachel, and Leah — recognize God, and however mixed their actions, they do His will.

Genesis 32

ANOTHER CRISIS in Jacob's life. A fresh and startling revelation of God.

Verses 1, 2: God's messengers. Before meeting Esau, God meets him, with the assurance of protection (28:12; 31:11). The ministry of angels is clear (Psa. 34:7; Dan. 6:22; Heb. 1:14). Jacob recognizes God's hand in this, and the word Mahanaim, "two hosts," refers to God's host of angels and his own host of possessions.

Verses 3-6: Man's messengers. Jacob realizes his need of being right with Esau, but his obsequiousness is unworthy of a man who trusts in God. The news of his brother's coming with armed men disconcerts him, and shows him that Esau remembered the past also.

Verses 7-12: Twofold fear. In verses 7, 8, Jacob fears man; in 9-12, he fears God. His prayer shows real but partial faith, and also true humility with intense earnestness. Grace is at work, though the stream of his life is not yet clear of unworthy elements.

Verses 13-23: Dread and distrust. Dread of man (vv. 13-19) and distrust of God (vv. 20-23). After prayer, planning again. He could not rely on God.

Verses 24-32: Divine discipline. Though Jacob's one thought was Esau, he had to meet God first, and in his solitude he finds an assailant. It was not Jacob wrestling with the angel, but the angel *with him.* The divine aim was to overcome Jacob's self-life, and the resistance was only overpowered by divine action, breaking down his opposition. When Jacob realized his helplessness, he ceased to strive and began to cling, and then came a threefold blessing: a new character (v. 28); a new power (v. 28); and a new experience, (v. 30). Then followed gratitude (v. 30) and glory around and within (vv. 31, 32).

Peniel, the Face of God (Exodus 33:11; Deut. 34:10), means Consecration, as Bethel, House of God, means Conversion. This was a new and a higher step for Jacob, as it always is for us. It includes (1) Character transformed; (2) Power assured; (3) Blessing received. Is this experience ours?

Genesis 33

WHY DOES THE NAME "Jacob" persist after Peniel? Because he went back from that position. He degenerated sadly.

Verses 1-11: First step backward. He still plots and plans, even after the assurance of power (32:28). The brothers meet, and Esau's opposition is seen to have been removed by God, but there is still fear and fawning on Jacob's part. All the recognition of God is by Jacob (vv. 5, 10, 11), but this is not on the level of Peniel.

Verses 12-17: Second step backward. After Esau's offer of escort was declined, Jacob promises to follow; but instead of going southeast, he goes directly opposite, northwest. This falsehood is absolutely inexcusable. What must Esau have thought when his brother did not arrive?

Verse 17: Third step backward. He did not stay for a time only, but made his home at Succoth. He had forgotten his vow at Bethel (28:21; 31:13). There were no pastures there, and he easily forgot God and his own word.

Verses 18-20: Fourth step backward. Still he did not go to Bethel, but on to a city of Shechem. Then he bought property there and was quite close to the Canaanites, a nearness which brought untold trouble. The altar was really a mockery. Devotion cannot make up for disobedience.

THE MESSAGE FOR MEDITATION

(1) Degeneration, even after consecration, is terribly possible to us. (2) Consecration can only be maintained by constant obedience. "I was not disobedient" — "Be thou faithful"!

Genesis 34

JACOB'S STAY at Succoth and Shechem extended over several years. Bethel and his vow had been forgotten (28:22). And this, after Peniel!

Verse 1: A grave peril is seen. Shechem had been selected largely for its favorable position for family and flocks. But the nearness to the Canaanites was a real danger. Bad society and weakened safeguards involve serious risks.

Verse 2: A great disaster follows. The inevitable result of nearness to Shechem was soon seen.

Verses 3-12: The proposition of reparation was at once suggested, for the man Shechem was evidently attached to Dinah. Why did Jacob keep silence? Was his conscience stirring?

Verses 13-17: The unworthy pretext of the brothers shows their character. Only on one condition could they entertain the proposal. The requirement seemed straightforward and natural. But their motive was wrong.

Verses 18-29: Trust and treachery, both were seen. The condition was accepted, but the object of the brothers was very different. Their religious pretence covered cruelty and vindictiveness.

Verses 30, 31: The rebuke and the rejoinder closed the incident for a time. Jacob's rebuke is feeble and selfish. No blame was given for the sin, but only a reference made to himself. The sons endeavored to justify their action, but omitted everything about their condition and its acceptance by Shechem.

THE MESSAGE FOR MEDITATION

(1) "In the world" means peril and powerlessness to believers, and calls for watchfulness. (2) "In the world but not of the world" means peace and protection, and always receives God's grace and blessing.

Genesis 35

THE STORY of a crisis.

Verse 1: The call. Bethel was only thirty miles away and yet it was ten years since Peniel. There was also the danger of the Canaanites seeking revenge.

Verses 2-4: The preparation. What a revelation of Jacob's toleration of evil! As the household saw he was in earnest, they made a complete surrender.

Verse 5: The journey. A remarkable testimony to the power of a life right with God.

Verses 6-8: The arrival. At once he acknowledges God. The name of the altar suggests his thought of God only, and not of self as in 33:20. Just then a link with the past was broken (v. 8).

Verses 9-15: The revelation and the response. Note "again," now that there was no cloud between Jacob and God. A fresh revelation and assurance and a grateful memorial followed. This is the first instance of a drink-offering.

Verses 16-20: Death. Sorrow was now to be the means of training, and after Deborah (v. 8) came the loss of his beloved Rachel. Again Jacob set up a pillar in memory of his love and sorrow.

Verses 21, 22: Sin. Another sorrow is the sin of his eldest son. But he met it in the strength of God ("Israel").

Verses 22-26: The list of sons — Reuben first and Benjamin last.

Verses 27-29: Another bereavement. There was no hindrance to Jacob's travel when once he had been to Bethel. Esau and Jacob met again. Did Esau think of his brother's deceit (33:14-17)?

THE MESSAGE FOR MEDITATION

(1) Discipleship is made real by "discipline." God often uses this to chasten and train us. (2) Discipline is made real by faith. The way to meet testing is to trust.

Genesis 36

Verses 1-8: Esau. Outwardly attractive, he was inwardly indifferent to God, and he lived quite regardless of those deeper realities which, with all his repulsiveness on the surface, Jacob fully recognized and valued. The two brothers were fitly separated (vv. 6, 7).

Verses 9-43: The line of Esau. Another illustration of the method of Genesis, the collateral branch being recorded first, and then dismissed.

THE MESSAGE FOR MEDITATION

When Hebrews 12:16 calls Esau a "profane person," it does not mean speaking profanity as today, but "secular," having no real idea of God in his life, no sacred spot which belonged to God, and where he might meet Him. Every true life will inevit-

ably find room for God and put Him first. "In the beginning,
God" (Gen. 1:1; see Proverbs 3:5-7).

Genesis 37

JOSEPH'S LIFE marks the last division of Genesis, though Jacob
is the head of the family. The narrative is very full, more being
recorded of Joseph than of any other patriarch.

Verses 1-4: Home life. Being about five or six when his
father left Mesopotamia, Joseph had escaped all the sad experiences of Jacob's earlier years at Haran. But the elder sons had
grown up in that atmosphere of jealousy and deceit, and they
resented their father's partiality to Joseph. They had no regard
for spiritual realities such as Joseph had, and his moral life
must have been a rebuke to them.

Verses 5-11: Dreams. These intensified the hatred. Jacob
was impressed even though he rebuked Joseph. The repetition
of the dream meant certainty of fulfillment (44:32).

Verses 12-17: The mission. Shechem was sixty miles from
Hebron, and the events of chapter 34 may have made Jacob
anxious. Joseph's obedience was prompt and thorough. He
combined all the best qualities of his ancestors: Abraham's ability,
Isaac's quietness, Jacob's capacity, Rachel's beauty (29:17;
39:6).

Verses 18-28: The brethren. The conspiracy was quickly and
cleverly planned, though Reuben proposed to rescue him. But
he was weak and irresolute, and soon the callous cruelty of the
rest was seen. Centuries after, this was recalled (Amos 6:6).
They were indifferent to his appeal (42:21). But an opportunity
came to enable them to avoid murder, and at the same time to
make some profit. Favorable circumstances are not always the
will of God.

Verses 29-36: Reuben's absence when needed probably indicated
his instability, together with his subsequent apparent acquiescence
in the plot. The father received the news with uncontrollable
grief, but meanwhile Joseph was safe in Egypt, even though in
slavery.

THE MESSAGE FOR MEDITATION

(1) The sin of envy is here sadly evident. It is the root of
every sin against our fellows (Psa. 37:1; 73:3; 1 Tim. 6:4; Prov.

14:30; James 3:16). (2) The grace of God alone can meet and master it (Psa. 37:3-7; 1 Peter 2:1).

Genesis 38

WHY IS THIS fearful story recorded here? Why is the record of Jacob and Joseph thus interrupted? There must have been a good reason. As this part of Genesis tells us of the transfer into Egypt through Joseph as the *instrument,* and by the divine power as the *cause,* so this terrible recital shows the *need* of it in the moral condition of Judah. The perils through contact with the Canaanites were so great that it was impossible to preserve the pure family of Jacob unless removed from contamination. The trouble was due to association with the people of Canaan, and this was following his father's example (chap. 34). It is not surprising that fearful results followed this sin.

THE MESSAGE FOR MEDITATION

(1) The terrible possibilities of sin are clearly suggested. Judah's life had been associated with good as well as with evil influences, and yet he fell. Shall we not ponder the plague of our own heart? (2) The absolute necessity of separation. Egypt was essential to the purity of the family of Jacob, and so the sale of Joseph was overruled for good. God's call is to separation (2 Cor. 6:17, 18). (3) The perfect righteousness of God. How frank and fearless is the Bible! Sin is sin by whomsoever committed. (4) The marvellous power of grace. (See Heb. 7:14 and Matt. 1:3). Only God could have done this. Grace forgives, uplifts, transmutes, and transforms. Sin abounds, but grace superabounds.

Genesis 39

EACH CHAPTER will now reveal some aspect of Joseph's character.

Verses 1-6: Prosperity. The young slave was faithful and thorough, with no complaint or murmuring. God therefore honored him. True prosperity is due to the presence and blessing of God.

Verses 7-12: Peril. Fierce temptation came to test him, but he met it with the threefold force of mind, conscience, and will. Duty to his master and loyalty to God were the two dominating principles. But temptation persisted, and Joseph saw that flight was the only safety, as it always is from certain forms of evil enticement. Then came the transformation of sinful love into equally sinful hate. But no one need sin. We can be pure, and shall be victorious if only we meet temptation as Joseph did.

Verses 13-23: Prison. Slander for a time conquered, but that victory was only temporary. Joseph's silence is remarkable as he bore the calumny and made no attempt at self-defense. But four times we read, "The Lord was with him," and the results were soon seen. By faithfulness he won the confidence of the jailer, just as he had done with his master, and proved the truth of the word, "Them that honor Me, I will honor."

THE MESSAGE FOR MEDITATION

(1) "Sweet are the uses of adversity." It is easy to say this, but not so easy to accept it in practice. Joseph bore three yokes: slavery, temptation, and slander; but it proved good for him, and revealed his integrity, prompted his growth, and prepared him for future opportunity. (2) The one great secret in adversity is trust in the presence, power, and justice of God. Psalm 37:6 is sure to follow our exercise of faith, as in v. 5; and Romans 8:28 will be proved true in every life.

Genesis 40

Verses 1-4: Working. The hand of God is seen in daily life. The two men to whom Joseph was servant proved a link in the chain of providence. Joseph was faithful, while silent about his troubles.

Verses 5-19: Watching. Joseph's quickness in seeing the perplexity of his fellow prisoners shows his unselfish concern for others. Then came his inquiry, their answer and his testimony to God. "Faithful in a very little" was Joseph's secret of life. In the interpretation of the first dream he reveals a human touch as he refers to himself. The words show what he felt amid his silence. The second dream was interpreted with equal frankness. Joseph did not swerve from the pathway of truth.

Verses 20-23: Waiting. Then came disappointment and two years of waiting. What a test it was! And yet it was probably the foundation of all the self-control that he showed later on.

THE MESSAGE FOR MEDITATION

Let us try to see God in the ordinary life of His children, in their sufferings, sorrows, disappointments, and difficulties. If we do, we shall realize that (1) God's way is wisest; (2) God's time is best; (3) God's love is certain; (4) God's grace is ample (James 1:4; Heb. 10:36).

Genesis 41

A WONDERFUL illustration of Romans 8:28.

Verses 1-7: The King's Dreams. This section is essentially Egyptian in character, and affords an opportunity of testing the truthfulness of the record. At no period after the life of Moses could so true an account of Egyptian life have been written, out of Egypt, by an Israelite. The dreams were associated with the Nile and the needs and condition of the land.

Verse 8: The Magicians' Failure. Notwithstanding the many opportunities afforded for these men to provide information of value to rulers, they were powerless at this juncture. Though the coloring of the dreams was Egyptian, they completely failed Pharaoh in regard to an explanation.

Verses 9-13: The Butler's Recollection. The law of association is a little thing, but it can produce wonderful results.

Verses 14-16: The Prisoner's Call. What a picture! The mighty monarch and the unknown slave. Joseph soon showed Pharaoh he was not like one of the magicians. The true explanation was at once forthcoming: "Not in me — God." His one thought was God's glory. "None of self, and all of Thee."

Verses 17-36: The Prisoner's Interpretation. The double dream meant certainty (v. 32). Joseph's counsel was wholly independent of himself, and his character stands out here with splendid force: integrity, conscientiousness, diligence, nobility, courage.

Verses 37-45: The Interpreter's Reward. Pharaoh quickly saw the value of this advice, and, further, that Joseph was the man for the work (v. 38, cf. Num. 27:18; Dan. 5:11). The Spirit of God is the source of practical powers, as well as of moral and spiritual gifts. He is for secular as well as for sacred life (Acts 6:3). The proofs of Joseph's appointment followed. "Bow the knee" is the rendering of "Abrek." In modern Egypt, camel-drivers say "Ibrik," when they want their camels to kneel, and slave mistresses use it to female slaves when ordered on their knees as a sign of repentance. "Zaphnath-paaneah" is of uncertain meaning, some suggesting "revealer of secrets," others "support of life." The wife given to Joseph is a further proof of his thorough identification with Egypt.

Verses 46-52: Joseph's public work and his home-life further reveal the remarkable changes.

Verses 53-57: A summary of the fourteen years, to be taken up in detail later (chap. 47).

THE MESSAGE FOR MEDITATION

(1) God has a purpose for the life of every one of His children. Joseph was led to his proper place. (2) God often uses unlikely circumstances to prepare us for our place. All Joseph's years in Egypt ministered to this. (3) God only asks us to be faithful to Him, whether in adversity or prosperity. (4) God will honor His servants who are true to Him, and "worketh for him that waiteth for Him" (Isa. 64:4, A.S.V.).

Genesis 42

MORE LINKS in the chain of God's providence.

Verses 1-5: Jacob's appeal to his hesitating and perplexed sons. Were their memories of Egypt troubling them? But family need soon overcame all else.

Verses 6-25: The meeting of the brethren with the great governor of Egypt. An unconscious fulfilment of the early dreams (37:7). As over twenty years had passed, Joseph's harshness was almost certainly intended as a test of their real character after so long a time. The demand for Benjamin was a further proof. Dr. A. T. Pierson once suggested to me the three elements of true repentance in v. 21: (1) Conscience "guilty"; (2) Memory "saw"; (3) Reason, "therefore." Reuben little knew that Joseph understood everything. The order about the money (v. 25) clearly shows the entire absence of revengeful feelings.

Verses 26-38: The return home was rudely interrupted, but v. 28 shows for the first time their recognition of God. A third test was then applied (v. 33). When they reached home, there was no deception of their father, as before.

THE MESSAGE FOR MEDITATION

(1) The power of conscience. After twenty years, and by a chain of simple events, all was brought back to these men. (2) The proof of repentance. A change of mind issuing in a change of life. This is what we can see in Joseph's brethren. (3) The powerlessness of reason. Jacob looked at the visible, and said: "All these things are nothing to me." But when we look at things from God's standpoint, we can see that "all things are working together for good."

Genesis 43

Verses 1-14: The Great Need. The famine continuing, Jacob urged his sons to go again to Egypt. But Judah showed him the impossibility of going without Benjamin, and refused to go unless Benjamin went with them. A significant touch of the old Jacob was seen in the response: "Why did you tell him you had a brother? Why not have kept silence about it?" Then, in response to Judah's earnest and urgent appeal and solemn promise, Jacob consented. The same attempt to appease, which he had made with Esau, was here repeated, and sending them with the money found in their sacks, Jacob commended them to the God of Power (*El Shaddai*). In spite of the indications of faithlessness and fear, the patriarch recognized the divine will in all these circumstances.

Verses 15-34: The Notable Reception. The fear shown by the brethren is very striking, and indicates a real change of heart. Simeon was restored to them, and again, in bowing down to him, they fulfilled the early dreams of Joseph. How simple and natural the narration, and yet how wonderful was the manifestation of divine providence! The feelings of Joseph at the sight of Benjamin testify to his emotions at seeing "his mother's son."

THE MESSAGE FOR MEDITATION

The chapter is full of suggestions. (1) The recovery of faith by Jacob is a lesson much needed today. As long as he looked on the dark side, all was wrong; but as soon as he faced the facts and remembered that God was almighty, his faith regained its strength and victory followed. "This is the victory . . . our faith." (2) The power of fear in the brethren is most striking. From first to last, fear possessed them (Gen. 42:28; 43:18). God often uses fear to search, warn, and guide us.

Genesis 44

Verses 1-12: The Plan. The orders of Joseph were evidently intended to include provision for the needs of his brethren, and to afford an opportunity to test them. The exact way in which this divining cup was used is not known, although various methods are described by ancient historians. Joseph seems to have been in the habit of employing it. The brethren had not gone far before they were overtaken, and the facts of the case discovered. The protestations of innocence, and the readiness to accept proper punishment, are very striking proofs of their genuine change of heart. When the cup was found, the words of Judah are particularly significant. Did they mean that he considered Benjamin guilty? Or did they allude to their sin of years before? The words in the plural, "Thy servants," seem to suggest the latter. Joseph's purpose to keep Benjamin as a slave was a further test of his brethren.

Verses 13-34: The Intercession. A wonderful utterance, full of beauty and power. Note (1) its deferential tone (cf. dreams 37:8); (2) its simplicity of narration; (3) its pathetic reference to Jacob; (4) its heroic offer. It was a clear and convincing proof of an entire change of character. On the assumption of Benjamin's guilt, disgrace had come to them all, and instead of at once slaying Benjamin, and thereby clearing themselves of all complicity, they returned to Egypt, and actually did not even reproach Benjamin. At last they were united and were ready to suffer together.

THE MESSAGE FOR MEDITATION

(1) The need of repentance. Joseph's testing was to discover whether the brethren had changed. God's testings of us are to see how far our lives are ready to respond to His will. His blessings cannot be ours until and unless we are prepared to turn from sin and wholly trust and follow Him. (2) The proof of repentance. The remarkable change in Judah (after 37:26 and 38:2) shows how the Spirit of God had been at work, eliciting

self-sacrifice and deepening his character.   Discipline was training
him, and so it will be with us.

Genesis 45

JOSEPH'S TESTS of his brethren having proved satisfactory, there
was no need of further delay in making himself known to them.

Verses 1-8: The Revelation.   The intensity of Joseph's feelings demanded privacy.   The revelation was met with silence
and fear, but Joseph soon reassured them.   It is very striking
that not a word of reproach fell from him, but assurance that
everything had been providentially ordered.

Verses 9-13: The Remembrance.   At once came Joseph's thought
for his father, and as the famine had still five years to run, Jacob
was urged to come down into Egypt.

Verses 14-15: The Reconciliation.   Tears of joy were shown
on both sides, and the phrase "all his brethren" is significant,
showing the full forgiveness.

Verses 16-24: The Reception.   Pharaoh's pleasure and invitation indicate a generous attitude.   He was probably Semitic,
one of the Shepherd Kings, and therefore partial to those of the
same race as his own.

Verses 25-28: The Result.   The news was almost incredible,
but Jacob's old weakness and partiality for something tangible
and not merely verbal asserted themselves, and "when he saw
the wagons" he fully believed and determined to go.   The exact
words of the text are striking: "The spirit of *Jacob* revived;
and *Israel* said . . . . "   The real man of God asserted himself.

THE MESSAGE FOR MEDITATION

A beautiful symbol of Christ's revelation to us: (1) Its method
— love's privacy; (2) Its power — love's pardon; (3) Its fulness
— love's peace; (4) Its assurance — love's provision.   All that
is needed is that this revelation of reconciliation should first be
believed and then told to others.

Genesis 46

NOTWITHSTANDING the great detail about Joseph, Jacob is still
the head of the family, and everything in the record is subservient

to the development of the divine purpose concerning him and his
house.

Verses 1-7: The Journey. Note the increasing references to
"Israel" rather than "Jacob" in this later period. The great
change needed special divine assurances (vv. 2-4). Beersheba
had many memories and associations (21:33; 22:19; 26:23;
28:10). God called him by his old name and used it twice. There
are ten of these duplications: 22:11; 46:2; Exod. 3:4; 1 Sam.
3:10; Luke 10:41; 22:31; Acts 9:4; Matt. 7:21, 22; 23:37;
Mark 15:34. God revealed Himself by a twofold name, "the
Mighty One" (El) and "the God of thy father," and a fourfold
promise was given. This extends far beyond the temporal circumstances of going into Egypt for food, because the real meaning
of this journey and change was the transformation of the family
into a nation. Room was needed to grow, preservation from
the Canaanites was essential, and not least, these pastoral men
would experience Egyptian civilization and government.

Verses 8-27: The Family. This list, appropriately inserted here,
includes some born in Egypt. "Seventy" suggests completeness,
and is a reminder of the seventy Jewish elders and Christ's seventy
disciples.

Verses 28-30: The Meeting. This loving reunion is one of the
most beautiful episodes in Scripture. Jacob's happiness was complete (v. 30).

Verses 31-34: The Plans. Joseph's action was at once marked
by principle and prudence. He must get Pharaoh's sanction,
and he would avoid any contact to which the Egyptians would
object. The feelings of the Egyptians about shepherds was probably due to the domination of the intruding Shepherd Kings.
Or else it was because of feeling that shepherds were of an impure
and inferior caste.

THE MESSAGE FOR MEDITATION

As we review Jacob's life in the light of these events, we see
(1) The greatness of God's purpose. God kept Jacob's family
long after the famine was over, using the circumstances of their
need to further His wider plans. "Thy judgments are a great
deep." (2) The reality of God's guidance. Step by step Jacob
and Joseph were led, whether they knew it or not. (3) The wis-

dom of God's love. In spite of all difficulties, Jacob could at length see the love that had been with him.

Genesis 47

Verses 1-6: The Complete Provision. Why five brethren only? Was this number significant among the Egyptians (43:34; 45:22)? The graciousness of Pharaoh is seen here as elsewhere in this story.

Verses 7-10: The Notable Interview. The patriarch blessing the king is a very striking illustration of Hebrews 7:7. He was thereby representative of his God. Jacob's comparison of himself with his father and grandfather, and his reference to his own life, are noteworthy for their pathos.

Verses 11, 12: The Special Care. At the king's word, Joseph placed his father and brethren "in the best of the land," and nourished them "according to the little ones," and thus, as the Hebrew suggests, the children were not forgotten. For the remaining five years of famine all would be well.

Verses 13-26: The Wise Ruler. This detail comes after the summary of 41:53-57, the story having been interrupted to deal with the coming of Joseph's brethren and the consequences, the narrative covering 42:1 to 47:12. Yet even here the Egyptian policy is looked at from Israel's standpoint, for the record is inserted between two sections (vv. 11, 12, and v. 27) which deal with the patriarch. Joseph's plan for the years of famine is fully stated. Its wisdom has been challenged as putting the people at the mercy of the crown, but they were tenants rather than slaves. The result was safety for the people and an extension of the influence of Egypt. Then, too, the purposes of God for Israel were thereby fulfilled, and the people kept safe and given opportunity to develop.

Verses 27-31: The Solemn Requirement. This was twelve years after the close of the famine. God must have indicated His will for the people to remain in Egypt.

THE MESSAGE FOR MEDITATION

Let us note the qualities that marked Joseph's public life: (1) Discreetness; (2) Promptness; (3) Thoroughness. They represent the three elements of personality: mind, heart, and will. And they come from God (chap. 41:38). Goodness is not incompatible with intellect and executive ability.

Genesis 48

Verses 1-7: The Striking Decision. The adoption of Ephraim and Manasseh into the family of Jacob is very remarkable. They were thus separated from Egypt and its prospects as the sons of the prime minister, and included in the people of God. It must have been a real test for them.

Verses 8-16: The Special Blessing. The threefold testimony to God was followed by a benediction covering their spiritual and temporal life. Scripture shows clearly the complete fulfillment of this.

Verses 17-22: The unusual action of Jacob (v. 14) was naturally a concern to Joseph, but his effort to change it was fruitless. Genesis is marked by a passing-over of the first-born: Seth instead of Cain; Shem instead of Japheth; Abraham instead of Haran; Isaac instead of Ishmael; Jacob instead of Esau. Thus the sovereignty of the divine will is seen here as throughout Scripture. And so Joseph does not appear in the list of his father's sons, but, instead, his own sons take his place. Another expression of Jacob's faith and hope, and a word about Joseph himself, closed this interview.

Verse 22: This seems to refer to an incident in Jacob's life not otherwise known.

The Message for Meditation

A beautiful picture of godly old age: (1) Faith looking upward; (2) Gratitude looking backward; (3) Love looking outward; (4) Hope looking forward.

Genesis 49

This chapter marks the close of the patriarchal dispensation, and the commencement of the development of the family into the nation. Jacob foresees and foretells the course of future events, especially as they should be brought about by the character of the sons.

Verses 1, 2: The Certainty of the Fulfillment. Jacob is a prophet.

Verses 3-27: The Variety of the Pronouncements. There are two main groups: one of six sons associated with Judah (vv. 3-18); and the other of four with Joseph (vv. 19-27). The accuracy of the fulfilment is remarkable when viewed in the light of what subsequently happened. Everything we know confirms the belief that Jacob spoke by divine inspiration. But the prophecies go far beyond the temporal history of the nation. They include some definite Messianic and spiritual elements (vv. 10, 18, 24, 25). In this revelation of God lay the secret of Israel's uniqueness and the guarantee of Israel's blessing.

Verses 28-33: The Closing Scene. With the definite blessing of the sons came a solemn charge. Jacob's mind was full of the promise of God. The description of his death is significant. He yielded his spirit to God, and was reunited to his forefathers. This is a clear proof of a belief in a future life.

THE MESSAGE FOR MEDITATION

(1) The solemnity of life as indicated by the faithfulness of the patriarch's words to his sons. (2) The splendor of life as revealed by the reference to God's relations to His people. (3) The satisfaction of life as seen in the attitude of Jacob to God in his last words of expectation.

Genesis 50

Verses 1-6: The Filial Love. Joseph's loss was great and deeply felt. The embalming was at once true to Egyptian custom and to Jacob's charge. The act indicated a belief in a future life with the soul reunited to the body.

Verses 7-14: The Complete Obedience. The great respect paid to Jacob is evident from the funeral procession and the action of Pharaoh. The oath of Joseph was fulfilled (47:29, 30), and is a fresh indication of the deep impression made by the divine promises.

Verses 15-18: The Surprising Fear. After years of fellowship, the brothers bring up what might have been thought forgotten. Their sense of guilt is most impressive. Weakness finds it difficult to believe in nobility. They measured Joseph by themselves. Their plea was twofold: their father's memory and their own attitude.

Verses 19-21: The Re-asserted Forgiveness. Once again Joseph had been misunderstood and mistrusted. But unspoiled and unsoured by all his experiences, he reassured them, reminded them of God's overruling providence, begged them to banish their fears, and pledged himself to take care of them.

Verses 22-26: The Persistent Faith. Fifty-four years were between verses 21 and 22, but neither daily duty nor family joys could remove from Joseph his steadfast faith. Like his father, he charged his brethren, and at length died.

THE MESSAGE FOR MEDITATION

(1) The presence of faith is seen in the oath required from the brethren. (2) The prospect of faith is seen in the expectation of the future. (3) The power of faith is seen in the consciousness of God realized by Joseph (v. 24).

4

THE BOOK OF EXODUS

INTRODUCTION

I. THE TITLE

The name "Exodus" comes from the Greek Version of the Old Testament and means "The Way Out," but the title of the book in the original Hebrew, taken from part of the first verse. reads "And these are the names." Clearly the book is a part of the Pentateuch even though a distinct section in itself, and the actual exodus recounted is but a part of the whole.

II. THE PURPOSE

As Genesis is the record of the Covenant made with the Patriarchs, so Exodus is the record of the Renewal and Perpetuation of that Covenant with the nation. Exodus contains the beginnings of Israel's national existence. The growth from the family to the nation is briefly passed over because the four centuries contained nothing of religious importance to narrate. But the increase and development were going on, and Exodus is the fulfillment of Genesis 50:24. As marking the opening stages of the national life, as Genesis does the individual, it is evident that Exodus is a continuation of Genesis.

It will easily be seen that the dominant note of the book is deliverance or redemption, in three aspects.

1. The Source and Instrument of Redemption — God through Moses (chaps. 1 to 6).

2. The Need and Fact of Redemption — Bondage and Passover (chaps. 7 to 12).

3. The Outcome and Object of Redemption — Salvation, Separation, and Service (chaps. 13 to 40).

III. THE CONTENTS

The purpose of the book is further and more fully seen by the actual contents, which consist of an introduction and three parts.

1. *Introduction.* — General Preparation, chapters 1 and 2.
   a. The People prepared for Deliverance (chap. 1).
   b. The Deliverer prepared for the People (chap. 2).
2. *Part* 1. — Preparation for the Covenant, chapters 3:1 to 18:27.
   a. Deliverance prepared (chaps. 3 to 6). The Preparation.
   b. Deliverance effected (chaps. 7 to 12). The Power.
   c. Deliverance confirmed (chaps. 13 to 18). The Protection.
3. *Part* 2. — Provision of the Covenant, chapters 19 to 34.
   a. Its Institution (chaps. 19 to 24). The Teaching.
   b. Its Continuance (chaps. 25 to 31). The Tabernacle.
   c. Its Breach (chaps. 32 to 34). The Testing.
4. *Part* 3. — Perpetuation of the Covenant, chapters 35 to 40.
   a. Instructions for building the Tabernacle (35:1-36:7).
   b. Material prepared (36:8 to 39:43).
   c. Erection accomplished (chap. 40).

Thus the purpose is shown by the structure of the book, and the national beginnings are seen in the nation being called by God (chaps. 1 to 12), led out, and then constituted and organized at Sinai (chaps. 13 to 18), and consecrated to God by means of the regular worship at the Tabernacle, the place of His presence (chaps. 19 to 40).

IV. The Types

Like Genesis, Exodus is valuable for its anticipation of higher and spiritual truths. But Genesis is largely concerned with personal types in the various men from Adam onwards, while Exodus is typical in its history as well.

1. Persons. Moses and Aaron. Cf. Hebrews 3:1, "Apostle and High Priest."

2. Places. Egypt (world); Red Sea (power).

3. Things. Lamb (redemption); herbs (discipline); pillar (protection); manna (food); rock (drink); tabernacle (presence of God).

4. The History in general (1 Cor. 10:6, 11).

V. The Message

The keynote is Redemption (3:8; 15:13; 19:4).
1. The Need — Egypt a type of the slavery of sin.

2. The Plan — Separation and Sacrifice; Repentance and Faith.

3. The Outcome — Victory, Protection, Provision, Guidance, Testing, Instruction, Worship.

CHAPTER STUDIES

Exodus 1

Verses 1-6: Recapitulation and advance of narrative. "And" links Exodus with Genesis, and carries the record forward from the original migration (see Gen. 35:22-26; 46:27; 50:26). The remarkable growth here indicated should be noted.

Verses 7-14: The multiplication and its results. The start of the history of Israel as a nation is here recorded. From the family had come a people. The rapid growth indicates a vigorous race. The new king was of a fresh dynasty. No hint is given of the time, the main point of the story being religious, not merely chronological. The "treasure-cities" were places for the storage of food and arms. The name of one, Rameses, suggests the Pharaoh of that name, either Rameses I, or Rameses II. The severity of the treatment did not produce the results expected. God was at work on behalf of His people, even though this fact is not mentioned. Prosperity with discipline is better than prosperity without it.

Verses 15-22: Failure of the first plan led to a second. But this also failed. Then came a still more terrible command (v. 22), addressed to all the people. The persistent opposition of Pharaoh is significant.

THE MESSAGE FOR MEDITATION

(1) God's power as seen in the wonderful increase of Israel. (2) God's purpose as seen in the preservation of Israel. (3) God's plan as seen in the permission of severe discipline to Israel. Nothing will be allowed to prevent the accomplishment of God's will. His purpose is unchangeable, and "the Lord will perfect that which concerneth" His own. Discipline will develop character while grace upholds (Isa. 43:2).

Exodus 2

Verses 1-10: Birth and Early Years of Moses. Amram was his father and Jochebed his mother (6:20). The narrative is full of Egyptian color.   "Flags" are reeds or other water-plants.[1] Pharaoh's daughter was perhaps a sister of Rameses II. Miriam's action was strikingly tactful and accomplished exactly what had been planned. The training of Moses is mentioned in Acts 7:20.

Verses 11-15: First Effort of Moses and its Failure.   His mother's influence had borne fruit, and Moses had determined to cast in his lot with Israel (Heb. 11:24), and now at forty he tries to help his afflicted brethren.   But he failed, God's time having not come, the divine call and authorization being wanting. The immediate result was flight.   Midian was probably to be identified with the present Sinaitic peninsula.

Verses 16-22: Reuel, or Jethro, was like Melchizedek, a survivor of the true worshippers, for he exercised priestly functions (18:12).   And so Moses found himself in very different circumstances, waiting instead of working; but "the keeping of sheep was the making of Moses." In Egypt he had learned to be "somebody"; in Midian he had to learn to be "nobody." It takes more strength to be patient than to act.

Verses 23-25: Israel's Continued Discipline.   The death of Pharaoh (perhaps Seti, father of Rameses II) made no difference to Israel, and we notice (1) their plight, and (2) their prayer. Then four things are said about God: He heard, remembered, looked, had respect.

THE MESSAGE FOR MEDITATION

(1) Faith, as seen in the parents of Moses.   (2) Failure, as seen in the impulsive effort of Moses.   (3) Faithfulness, as seen in the response of God to Israel.   Notice also the splendid statements about Moses in Hebrews 11:23-27.

Exodus 3

Verses 1-10: The Call of Moses.   The bush burning and yet not consumed was not a type of Israel in affliction and yet not destroyed.   It was a symbol of God, His presence and power. It also told of His character of holiness (v. 5) and His faithfulness to His promises.   God's action was a reminder that He is always first, and that He was about to deliver His people. The double call implied urgency, as in 1 Samuel 3:10 and else-

---

1. Another name sometime used for iris.

where, ten times altogether. The response of Moses was followed by a full revelation of the Divine relationship to Moses and to Israel (v. 6), and then came a fourfold statement of the divine attitude: seen, heard, known, come down. The work would be twofold: to "deliver out" and to "bring up into." On this firm basis Moses was summoned to be God's instrument.

Verses 11-15: Hesitation met by Assurance. The reluctance was natural, but God gave a twofold promise (v. 12). All the old rashness (chap. 2) had gone, and the request for a full explanation of the mission, if asked for by the people, was granted by the revelation of God as the One who is ever the same in His real, unchanging, and eternal nature. "I Am" (v. 14) and "Jehovah" (v. 15) have the same meaning of the ever-present, ever the same, the unchangeable God of the covenant (see Rev. 1:4, 8; 4:8; 11:17; 16:5). Then came the identification of this "I Am" with the God of their fathers as a further assurance. Thus, two difficulties are met, one about Moses himself (vv. 11, 12), and the other about God (vv. 13, 14), and revelation overcame (at least for a time) reluctance. Notice how Christ used this name "I am" of Himself (John 8:58).

Verses 16-22: The Commission. Two messages are to be delivered: first, one to the elders of Israel (v. 16), and then, the other to Pharaoh (v. 18). God's promise of deliverance is accompanied by a clear revelation of Egypt's unwillingness, but in spite of this the assurance is given of the certain accomplishment of the divine purpose.

Verse 22: "Borrow" is in the Hebrew, "ask," as in Judges 5:25; 1 Kings 3:11; 2 Kings 2:10. Israel had a right to this payment after their slavery. It was compensation freely given: there was no fraud or deceit.

THE MESSAGE FOR MEDITATION

(1) "The Lord is mindful of His own"; (2) "God is able to make all grace abound"; (3) "More than conquerors."

Exodus 4

Verses 1-9: The first difficulty was the probable unbelief of the people. This was met by the two signs, giving God's full assurance.

Verses 10-12: The second difficulty was the lack of the speaking faculty felt by Moses. This was met by the divine promise of guidance and power.

Verses 13-17: The third stage. Moses' continued reluctance and request for someone else. This was met by God's condescension to send Aaron along with him. Thus Moses lost God's first choice. Aaron was never originally intended; Moses was to go alone. But he shrank from this, and then had to take God's "second-best." Aaron was often a trouble and weakness to him (32:21).

Verses 18-23: Return to Midian, and permission sought of the head of the nation or tribe. God's renewed command, with the solemn warning to Pharaoh, anticipating the tenth plague.

Verses 24-26: Moses had evidently neglected the divine command (Gen. 17:9-14), probably having yielded to his Midianitish wife, who was out of sympathy with him. But in view of his work it was essential that he should have everything right, especially as the nation of Israel would rightly expect obedience to this ordinance. God's workers cannot afford to leave any command unheeded. "Be ye clean that bear the vessels of the Lord" (Isa. 52:11).

Verses 27-31: Moses' wife and children apparently returned to Midian (18:2), and he went on to Egypt, where he first met Aaron, and then the elders, and the credentials were presented in proof of the divine commission. The response was (1) trustful and (2) thankful.

THE MESSAGE FOR MEDITATION

(1) The absolute assurance of victory in spite of hesitation. (2) The utter sadness, in not taking God at His word, of losing His best and highest blessings. (3) The essential duty of putting God first, and of laying aside every weight and all disobedience, if we are to be used of Him (Heb. 12:1; Luke 14:26, 27, 33).

Exodus 5

Verses 1-5: First interview with Pharaoh. Everything settled with Israel (4:30, 31), the next step was to request permission from Pharaoh to leave Egypt. The attitude of the king to God was probably due to pretended ignorance based on wilfulness.

Fresh reasons followed the first refusal, and to these Pharaoh made no direct reply, but charged Moses and Aaron with hindering the people from doing their proper work. The inaction of so many meant heavy loss to the nation.

Verses 6-9: Additional work was imposed so as to prevent any further objectionable demands. Pharaoh planned to push Israel by requiring the same quantity of bricks without supplying the necessary straw or stubble. They were to gather it for themselves, and yet provide the exact number of bricks as before. Thus, they would be kept quiet and agitation would cease.

Verses 10-14: The effort to obey this severe demand proved a failure, and though they were beaten (probably by bastinadoes or type of baton, or stick, applied to the soles of the feet, an Eastern form of punishment), the task was impossible.

Verses 15-19: An appeal to the king was fruitless, for the people were charged with laziness and hypocrisy.

Verses 20-21: Then the people vented their indignation on Moses and Aaron, charging them with being the cause of all the trouble.

Verses 22, 23: Without any reply to the people, Moses and Aaron told God about the trouble, and in evident discouragement complained that the promised deliverance (3:8, 20) had not come.

THE MESSAGE FOR MEDITATION

Three lessons: (1) Wilful ignorance of God (v. 2) inevitably leads to injustice to man (vv. 6, 7). The brotherhood of man is only possible on the basis of the Fatherhood of God through the Saviorhood of Jesus Christ. (2) "Sweet are the uses of adversity," though we may not realize this at once (Heb. 12:11). (3) "Take it to the Lord in prayer" (v. 22) is the best way of meeting troubles and difficulties.

Exodus 6

Verses 1-8: God's reply. New encouragement was given, based on the character of God Himself as the Covenant God, and therefore the ever-present and unchangeable One. Thus 3:13-15 was repeated for confirmation, and with this assurance, promises were given which were to be passed on. Note the aspects of the revelation: "I am"; "I have"; "I will." Also the seven "I wills."

Verse 3 indicates that while the name "Jehovah" was used in old days (e.g., Gen. 4:26; 22:14), its meaning was not fully known. Its real and full interpretation was now to be understood as the eternal, unchangeable dependable God of His people.

Verse 9: The people were too depressed and disheartened to be helped by these glorious assurances. Both body and spirit were suffering.

Verses 10-12: The second challenge to Pharaoh. Moses hesitated to make another effort. Self-distrust (4:10) arose again.

Verse 13: A summary of chapters 3 to 5 prefixed to the genealogy.

Verses 14-27: A genealogical section. The family history is taken up from 1:5. Israel's life was founded on tribal relationships, and the list is inserted here just before the crisis in Egypt, and probably as a prelude to the work of Moses and Aaron (v. 26).

Verses 28-30: Then comes a resumption of the history from v. 12, almost a repetition.

THE MESSAGE FOR MEDITATION

Let us concentrate on God as recorded in this chapter. (1) What He is. "I am Jehovah" (vv. 2, 3). (2) What He has done (vv. 4, 5). (3) What He will do (vv. 6-8). Thus the past (2) and the future (3) are based on the present (1), on the character of God Himself (see Mal. 3:6). This is the true answer to despair (v. 9) and distrust (v. 12).

Exodus 7

Verses 1-7: The divine assurance before the conflict opens. "Prophet" means "spokesman," one who represents another. There is no longer any hesitation or wavering on the part of Moses. Henceforward he proceeds step by step with the fearlessness of faith in God. "Harden" (v. 3) is the expression, not of the divine purpose but of the result of disobedience to the divine appeals. As a matter of fact, all the plagues were intended and calculated to soften, if Pharaoh had been willing to yield. Very often, however, the result of man's wilfulness is attributed in Scripture to the divine will, just as we may say of a man burning himself, either that he did it or that God did it, because it was due to a divine law of nature that the result accrued.

Verses 8-13: The First Sign. This was a failure. The Egyptian magicians were permitted by God to imitate this action of Moses. Serpents were often charmed and stiffened like rods. See 2 Tim. 3:8. But a superiority is clearly shown. The permission was doubtless for a test of Pharaoh and of Moses, the one as to obedience, the other as to trust.

Verses 14-21: The First Plague. Judgment began with the sacred river, the Nile, and from this the results extended to all other streams.

Verses 22-25: Again the magicians exercised their power. The water they used came from the wells referred to in verse 24. But it was in no sense what Moses had done, because the streams were already affected. Yet it was sufficient to make Pharaoh again determined to keep Israel.

THE MESSAGE FOR MEDITATION

(1) A prophet is one who represents God to man (v. 1) and, as such, all the Lord's people are prophets. Are we giving those around a true idea of God? (Acts 1:8). (2) The awful possibility of self-will when faced even with the clearest demonstration of God's presence and power. (3) The fearful power of Satan in deceiving people with counterfeits of the true (1 Tim. 2:14; 1 Kings 22:22).

Exodus 8

Verses 1-7: The Second Plague. Frogs were held sacred in Egypt, so that this plague would both demonstrate God's power, and also strike at one of the Egyptian forms of religion. The frogs could not be killed because of their sacredness, and yet such large numbers of them would be revolting in their loathsomeness, especially because cleanliness was a particular mark of the Egyptians. Once again, the magicians imitated the action of Aaron, but it is quite unknown how it was done, whether by sleight of hand or enchantment.

Verses 8-15: Pharaoh's Appeal. He acknowledges the power of the One he had professed not to know (5:2). Mark the specific promise to let Israel go (v. 8). "Glory over me" is probably an expression of courtesy, "I submit to thy will — have the honor of my submission" (Pulpit Commentary). Moses asks for what date he shall pray that the frogs may be removed, and the king's answer is that they should be removed on the next day. Moses accepts this, and tells Pharaoh it will be a proof of the power of Jehovah. When, however, the answer came, Pharaoh became hardened again, and did not fulfill his promise.

Verses 16-19: The Third Plague. This was one of lice or mosquitoes (the Greek Version favors the latter). The Hebrew word is found only here and in the Psalms which refer to this event (78:46; 105:31). It is known that mosquitoes are, and always have been, a very great trouble in Egypt. It is noteworthy that the magicians made no further effort to oppose Moses and Aaron. They recognized God at last. But Pharaoh still resisted.

Verses 20-24: The Fourth Plague. The nine plagues are in three groups of three each, two in each being preceded by a warning and the third without. The fourth is the first of the second series. The Hebrew word is thought to mean "fly" or "beetle," the latter being prevalent and troublesome in Egypt. The beetle, being sacred, would not be destroyed. This plague was to be a special proof of the distinction between the people of Israel and Egypt (vv. 22, 23).

Verses 25-32: Pharaoh was impressed, and proposed two compromises, the first in verse 25, and the second in verse 28. But these were impossible. The great necessity was separation from Egypt, the distance proving a safeguard. The former, involving the sacrifice of animals regarded by the Egyptians as sacred, would cause trouble; and the latter would have been dangerous, because too near Egypt. The three days (3:18) would not have taken them far enough away. But Moses did not object to this; he left the matter to God, and prayed for the removal of the plague. But again Pharaoh proved obdurate.

THE MESSAGE FOR MEDITATION

(1) The terrible power of wilful resistance to God. (2) The supreme authority of God to be recognized at all times. (3) The mercy of God intended to lead to repentance (Rom. 2:4). (4) The serious danger of any religious compromise, lest it sacrifice truth.

Exodus 9

Verses 1-7: The Fifth Plague. The earlier plagues chiefly attacked persons; this comes on property. The pestilence was an epidemic with which Egypt was familiar, though its miraculousness was seen in the circumstances of the time of its appearance, its severity, and its limitation to the Egyptian cattle. Apparently Pharaoh was scarcely moved by this visitation.

Verses 8-12: The Sixth Plague. The last of the second series, coming without warning. A terrible malady of some unknown kind came, and proved of intense severity. The reference to the magicians is emphatic and striking (v. 11). But even this had no effect on Pharaoh.

Verses 13-26: The Seventh Plague. Pharaoh was solemnly warned of this beforehand. The long message (vv. 13-19) is unique. Some Egyptians evidently believed Moses' word and Moses' God (v. 20). All this was done for the purpose that the surrounding nations might know of the one true God (v. 16). Note the boldness of Moses in contrast with his former hesitation. With verse 26 compare 8:22; 9:4; 10:23.

Verses 27-35: At length, Pharaoh was thoroughly roused. Death had come. The act was clearly supernatural (v. 26). So Pharaoh acknowledged his sin, and prayed for the removal of the infliction. Pharaoh's "I have sinned" (v. 27) is one of eight such confessions in Scripture, four sincere and four insincere. But no sooner had the plague ceased, than the king once more forgot his words, and hardened his heart against Israel. "The Lord God" or "Jehovah God" (v. 30) is found in the Pentateuch only here and in Gen. 2:4 to 3:23.

THE MESSAGE FOR MEDITATION

(1) The awful possibilities of persistent wickedness. (2) The splendid courage which comes from faith in God. (3) The shallowness of sorrow which is only concerned with escaping the consequences of sin.

Exodus 10

Verses 1-20: The Eighth Plague. Locusts (Joel 2:25) would complete the work that the hail had begun. The effect was profound. For the first time Egyptian officers pleaded with Pharaoh. The king was so far influenced as to propose a third compromise (vv. 8-11), but this was equally impossible. To leave the children behind would inevitably tend to bring back the parents to Egypt, and so Pharaoh would again have them as slaves.

The fearful effects of the plague led Pharaoh to send hastily for Moses and Aaron (v. 16). Notice verse 17, "only this once," which was true, for Pharaoh did not ask for any other plague to be removed. But, again, the removal of the trouble led to Pharaoh's refusing to let Israel go.

Verses 21-29: The Ninth Plague. The third of the third series was inflicted without any warning beforehand. The darkness was probably caused by an intensification of a natural Egyptian phenomenon, the wind storm which causes sand and dust to rise and darken the sun's rays. But as before, the marks of God's supernatural visitation are clear (vv. 21, 23). Pharaoh was so deeply impressed that he proposed a fourth compromise, but with courage and scorn Moses refused this. Then Pharaoh in anger put an end to the conference, and dismissed Moses, who readily accepted the dismissal.

THE MESSAGE FOR MEDITATION

(1) The limits of God's forbearance may be reached (v. 3; Prov. 1:28). (2) The hardening of the heart is possible in the face of even the greatest of God's manifestations. (3) The clear distinction between the "children of light" and the "children of darkness" (vv. 21-23). (4) Note the four compromises and their perils. The true attitude is "Not compromise at the expense of truth, but comprehensiveness for the sake of truth."

Exodus 11

Verses 1-3: The Announcement. Perhaps this refers to something that happened before (10:24). There was to be one more plague, and this would be effectual, for Pharaoh would be eager to send Israel away. "Borrow" is "ask," as in 3:22.

Verses 4-8: These verses seem to be the continuation of 10:29, at Moses' last interview with Pharaoh, and forming the solemn announcement before he left the presence of the king. The warning is very impressive. Moses was the divine instrument (v. 4), and the visitation would bring fearful results to Egypt (v. 6), while Israel would be entirely free (v. 7). In view of the law of primogeniture, the blow would be the most terrible that could be inflicted.

Verses 9, 10: A summary before approaching the last plague. God's wonders were intended to impress Egypt and other nations with His might and majesty. The nine plagues can now be seen as a whole. They touched every phase of nature: mineral, animal, vegetable, human. They affected persons and property, and included all, from the highest to the lowest.

THE MESSAGE FOR MEDITATION

The contrast in character between Moses and Pharaoh. (1) Trust in God contrasted with self-assertion. (2) Courage contrasted with stubbornness. (3) Consistency contrasted with changeableness. (4) Strength contrasted with weakness.

Exodus 12

Verses 1-13: The Instructions about the Passover. The crisis had come and the new festival was to mark a new beginning, the opening events of Israel's national life. The remarkable fulness of details in these instructions is very significant. The Passover was to be far more than the occasion of deliverance from Egypt; it was to be an integral part of Israel's life from that time. We may think of it as a revelation of God's love for the people, and the requirements show what God intended the people to learn and remember. The fact of sacrifice here emphasized, is an illustration of its prominence in Scripture from Genesis 4 onward. It meant redemption from sin.

Verses 14-20: The continuance year by year is ordered, thereby showing the permanence and prominence of the festival. The absence of leaven meant purity, another reminder of God's requirements.

Verses 21-28: The people were given these instructions, receiving them in an attitude of reverence, and at once put them into practice.

Verses 29-36: The Tenth Plague. Nine had produced no result, but this was so awful that it had immediate and effectual consequences. Pharaoh made a complete surrender, and Israel was promptly dismissed. It was a striking thing that Pharaoh sought Moses' blessing before he left (v. 32).

Verses 37-39: The departure was hurried and yet complete. With those who were impressed enough to go with them, the numbers are thought to be about two million.

Verses 40-42: Summary of the sojourn in Egypt. The date is from Jacob's arrival (Gen. 46).

Verses 43-51: Further supplementary directions about the Passover.

THE MESSAGE FOR MEDITATION

In the light of 1 Corinthians 5:7 and 1 Peter 1:18, 19, the Passover becomes luminous with spiritual meaning. (1) It speaks of perfect redemption from the peril and bondage of sin. (2) It declares God's requirement, and also His provision of a perfect sacrifice (John 3:16). (3) It tells of spiritual strength for life's journey by feeding on the Sacrifice (John 6:54-57). (4) It assures of absolute safety and complete certainty by the trustful acceptance of and obedience to the Word of God (Exod. 12:13, 27, 28). "The Blood secures; the Word assures."

Exodus 13

Verses 1-16: The New Life. After redemption comes consecration. Israel had been saved through the destruction of Egypt's first-born, and now they were required to dedicate their own first-born as a constant memorial of their deliverance. Not that the rest were exempt, but the first-born were, like the Sabbath day and the first ears of corn, a pledge of the dedication of the whole nation. The absence of leaven is again emphasized. Leaven is a symbol of evil. Thus, God claimed the best that Israel had. The first-born were intended as God's ministers, and though afterward the Levites were substituted for them (Num. 3:40-51; 18:16) the principle remained intact.

Verses 17, 18: God's leading naturally followed the deliverance from Egypt. He never forsakes His own.

Verse 19: In spite of the hurried departure, Moses did not forget the testimony of God's faithfulness which he always had before him in the mummy of Joseph (Heb. 11:22).

Verses 20-22: God's Miraculous Guidance. The first mention of the pillar of cloud and fire, clearly supernatural. See 14:19-24; 33:9; Numbers 12:5; 14:11. Mentioned last in Numbers 16:42; 20:6. (Cf. Neh. 9:19). No reference to it in Joshua. The characteristics were its clearness for guidance; its varied manifestations according to need; its permanence as long as Israel needed it on the journey. The miraculous was only granted when needed. All else was natural, because moral training was essential.

THE MESSAGE FOR MEDITATION

(1) Consecration is the natural and inevitable outcome of redemption. Romans 12 ("mercies of God") looks back to Romans 3:21-26 and Romans 8:31-39. (2) Wise love is seen in the way God led the inexperienced people (vv. 17, 18). His is always the "right way" (Psa. 107:7), even though it is not always the shortest (Deut. 32:10, "about"). (3) The perpetual presence of God is always the foundation, inspiration, and satisfaction of His people (Matt. 28:20; Gen. 28:15; Isa. 41:10; Matt. 1:23, "God with us").

Exodus 14

Verses 1-4: The Journey Continued. The change from southeast to south would keep them within Egypt's fertile lands, and prevent them from suffering the hardships of the desert, which they would have experienced if they had continued to the southeast.

Verses 5-9: But this change prompted Pharaoh to pursue, because Israel was thus between him and the sea. The "wilderness" referred to was that in Egypt, between the Nile valley and the Red Sea. Pharaoh had recovered from the effects of the last plague, and made another effort to retain Israel by recapture.

Verses 10-14: Israel's fear is in marked contrast with Moses' courage. The test was severe, but short memories might and should have been avoided. The untrained host would naturally be no match for the Egyptian army, but the supernatural was overlooked (v. 14).

Verses 15-18: God's Answer to Pharaoh's Effort. Force met by faith.

Verses 19-22: The Crossing by Israel. The divine action helped Israel and hindered Egypt, and the natural (v. 21) blended with the supernatural (1 Cor. 10:1, 2; Heb. 11:29).

Verses 23-31: The Destruction of the Egyptians. Thus, the words "no more for ever" (v. 13) were fulfilled. The narrative is not clear as to Pharaoh himself, but even if he perished, his body could have been recovered, and the mummy of Meren-ptah now in the Cairo Museum, may be that of the actual monarch.

THE MESSAGE FOR MEDITATION

(1) God's permissive discipline is to test and train His people. "As gold must be tried in the fire . . ." (2) God's method of deliverance was to put the Red Sea between Egypt and Israel. Christ's resurrection marks the gulf between sin and salvation, between peril and protection, between fear and faith (Rom. 5:8-10). (3) God's people always suffer by distrusting Him, while they ever honor Him, and also do themselves good, by taking Him at His word (John 11:40).

Exodus 15

Verses 1-18: The Song of Moses and Miriam. The first recorded poem of the nation. (1) Verses 1-12, retrospect, deliverance. Three direct addresses to "the Lord": 2-5; 6-10; 11-12. The first reference to God's holiness, in v. 11, meaning primarily (not purity, but) remoteness from earth — separation, transcendence. This is the root meaning of sanctification (Gen. 2:3), and a "holy place" is one set apart for sacred use. (2) Verses 13-18, prospect, anticipating results.

Verses 19-21: The facts related as a reason for the song. Miriam's part was a response. Compare the "Songs of Moses and the Lamb" (Rev. 15:2, 3).

Verses 22-27. The Journey Resumed. After the Red Sea came Marah, a further test. The forgetfulness of past mercies is sad, but familiar. Again, supernatural power was exercised. The circumstances were made a special occasion for a divine statute, promising exemption from disease on fulfilment of certain conditions. "It is a significant fact that at this day, after eighteen hundred years of oppression, hardship, and persecution, of the ghetto, and the old-clothes trade, the Hebrew people are proverbially exempt from repulsive and contagious disease. They also 'certainly do enjoy immunity from the ravages of cholera, fever, and smallpox in a remarkable degree. Their blood seems to be in a different condition from that of other people . . . They seem less receptive of disease caused by blood-poisoning than others' (*Journal* of Victoria Institute, xxi, p. 307). Imperfect as was their obedience, their covenant at least has been literally fulfilled to them" (Chadwick, *Exodus,* p. 230).

THE MESSAGE FOR MEDITATION

(1) The Theme of the Song is God as (a) Strength, (b) Song, (c) Salvation. Note these three in Psalm 118:14 and Isaiah 12:2. The third is the reason for the first, and the second is the outcome of both. God is, first, our Salvation, then our Strength, and then our Song. (2) The testimony of the Song is our attitude to God: (a) "My God," (b) "My father's God," (c) Resolutions: "I will prepare Him a habitation"; "I will exalt Him." (3) The Truth of the Song is God's work for His people (v. 13): (a) He has redeemed them; (b) He has led and guided them; (c) He has a place for them (Psa. 107:7, 30); (d) all is due to His "mercy" and "strength."

Exodus 16

Verses 1-3; Murmuring for Food. Deliverance wholly forgotten. Slavery in Egypt entirely overlooked. In view of all these sad manifestations, the deplorable spiritual state of the people can readily be seen. They had seriously deteriorated in Egypt.

Verses 4-8: God's Promise of Provision. Note again, as in 15:25, the word "prove."

Verses 9-21: The Food. Verse 15, "it is manna," is best rendered, "This is a gift," thus explaining the words that immediately follow. See Psalm 78:26.

Verses 22:30: The gathering on the sixth day, showing that the Sabbath was in existence before the delivery of the Law. See Genesis 2:3.

Verses 31-36: Summary, recording the appearance, a special use and the continuance of the manna. The "omer" is to be distinguished from the "homer."

THE MESSAGE FOR MEDITATION

(1) Grace alone can choose us to receive God's interest and salvation (Deut. 9:5-7). (2) The manna was a wonderful type of Christ (John 6.32), expressing both man's need and God's love. (3) Christ is the source, sustenance, and satisfaction of the Christian life. (4) The manna had to be both gathered and eaten. The appropriation of faith is essential (John 6:35). See Isaiah 55:2, "Hearken" (attention); "eat" (appropriation); "delight" (appreciation).

Exodus 17

Verses 1-7: The Second Murmuring for Water. At Marah (15:23) there was no drinkable water, but at Rephidim there was none at all. The persistent failure of the people was very disappointing. Their blame of Moses and their reference to Egypt were most unfair and bitter. But Moses took the trouble to God, and the outcome was another divine intervention. As a memory, he called the place Massah (test) and Meribah (strife).

Verses 8-16: War with the Amalekites. Amalek was grandson of Esau (Gen. 36:12), and although akin to Israel, proved their most inveterate foe, as the subsequent history shows (Num. 24:20; 1 Sam. 14:48; 15:7; 27:8; 30:17; 2 Sam. 8:12; 1 Chron. 4:41-43). This is the first mention of Joshua (Num. 13:8). The "rod of God" meant that a divine victory was expected, and the intercession (v. 11) indicates the same. The Book (v. 14) evidently existed already, and was the germ of our Old Testament. Sacrifice followed, and the altar, "Jehovah is my Banner," was a further acknowledgment of God. Amalek's sin was great in fighting God's people (Deut. 25:18), who were their own kin and were not prepared for the attack. Amalek had really fought against God.

THE MESSAGE FOR MEDITATION

(1) "Have we trial or temptation? . . . Take it to the Lord in prayer." (2) God has unexpected ways of provision. (3) Christ is the Water of Life: fresh, pure, abundant, suitable, accessible, unfailing (1 Cor. 10:4; John 7:37). (4) Amalek symbolizes the flesh, our nearest and closest foe, but victory is certain (Gal. 5:24; Rom. 7:18, 24, 25). (5) The mighty power of intercession, Christ's and ours (Heb. 7:25; Job 42:10; 2 Thess. 3:1).

Exodus 18

Verses 1-12: Jethro's Visit to Moses. The wife and sons of Moses had evidently been sent back to Midian (4:26). Some think Jethro was the brother-in-law of Moses (the word is equally capable of this rendering), Reuel being his father (3:1). Others think the two names refer to the same man. Jethro was evidently a follower of the true God, and was priest and head of his tribe, though he seems to have held the common idea of a plurality of gods, which he here renounces.

Verses 13-23: Jethro's Counsel. Jethro soon saw the heavy strain on Moses, who had not delegated any authority. So Jethro advised the appointment of associates as subordinate judges, with the reservation to Moses of the important cases. It was wise counsel.

Verses 24-26: The acceptance by Moses, and selection of the men for the work. Deuteronomy 1:13 indicates that the people actually made the selection.

Verse 27: Jethro's Return Home. This took place soon afterward. Numbers 10:29-32 is to be carefully distinguished from this incident, even if Hobab and Jethro are the same person. The elders of Numbers 11:14-17 are probably a divine confirmation and re-appointment of these elders.

THE MESSAGE FOR MEDITATION

(1) The recognition of God's power (vv. 1, 9, 10). (2) The recognition of God's supremacy (v. 11). (3) The recognition of God's presence (v. 12). (4) The recognition of God's work (vv. 15, 16). (5) The recognition of God's righteousness (v. 21), men of ability, piety, veracity, and sincerity. (6) The recognition of God's will (vv. 19, 23).

Exodus 19

Verses 1, 2: Summary of the Journey from Egypt to Sinai.

Verses 3-9: The First Covenant between God and the People. Moses is called into the presence of God and is commanded to tell Israel of the past (v. 4), the present (v. 5), and the future (v. 6). These verses are very important as indicating God's purpose with and through Israel. They were to be His special witnesses and representatives. A priest represents man to God (Heb. 5:1), and the nation of Israel were to be "priests" for the world. And holiness, meaning primarily separateness, was to mark this testimony. The people were deeply impressed and heartily responsive.

Verses 10-15: The Preparation for the Entrance into the Covenant. Since sanctification is primarily separation, this took the form of purification (vv. 10, 14). External features were symbolical and expressive of internal requirements.

Verses 16-20: The Divine Manifestation. See Deuteronomy 4:11, 12, for another description. Everything was intended and calculated to impress the people with the reality and majesty of the God with whom they were entering into covenant.

Verses 21-25: A further warning was felt to be necessary, even after what had already been said and done. Some think it was due to a genuine and warranted fear that they would presume and approach too close. Their former wilfulness and murmuring make this idea very possible. Had the priests failed to observe the command about sanctification (vv. 10, 22)? See Hebrews 12:18-25.

THE MESSAGE FOR MEDITATION

(1) The Covenant of God: based on redemption (v. 4); realized by obedience (v. 5); marked by privilege (v. 5); proved by uniqueness (v. 5); and expressed in duty (v. 6). (2) The Purpose of God. The people were to be "a kingdom of priests, a holy nation." They were thus to show to the world who and what God was. (3) The Character of God. The one thought is "holiness," meaning separation, transcendence — "God the infinitely-high." The corresponding aspect, "God the infinitely-nigh" is only possible in Christ (John 1:1, 18).

Exodus 20

Verses 1-17: The Ten Commandments. After the special preparations (chap. 19), came the delivery of the Decalogue ("Ten Words"), and a study of it shows that it is a perfect moral code, suited for all men, times, and circumstances. It was based on redemption (v. 2) and indicates man's twofold relation — to God and to those around him. The proper division is five and five, not four and six, because our parents (Fifth Commandment) are never regarded as equivalent to our equals (neighbors), but as God's representatives. The Fifth Commandment is, therefore, the transition between the two tables, and one phrase "the Lord thy God" (not found in the rest), links the first five together. (1) Verses 3-12, our relation to God: thoughts (vv. 3-6); words (v. 7); deeds (vv. 8-12). (2) Verses 13-17, our relation to man: deeds (vv. 13-15); words (v. 16); thoughts (v. 17). Thus, every element of life is met, and the emphasis on thoughts is seen by its prominence in the first and last commandments (Prov. 4:23).

Verses 18-21: The Effect on the People. Notice their "fear" of God and the "fear not" of Moses (v. 20); their distance and Moses' nearness (v. 21).

Verses 22-26: Special Reminders and Injunctions. God's revelation (v. 22) is followed by negative and positive commands: against idolatry, and concerning true worship. The instructions about the "altar" are threefold: it should be of earth, but if of stone, it was not to be of hewn stone, or to have steps approaching it. This means that the altar was to be natural, not artificial, because elaborate manufacture and carving were associated with idolatry. Decency, too (v. 26), was essential until the sacerdotal vestments were provided (38:3-43).

THE MESSAGE FOR MEDITATION

(1) The Divine Requirement. Obedience in thought, word, and deed; nothing less will suffice. (2) The Divine Reason. They were God's redeemed people (v. 2). (3) The Human Response. Awe and dread, because of God's holiness and majesty. (4) The Human Result. The Divine Assurance (v. 20) was to encourage them to obedience and the avoidance of sin. In the power of the Spirit the redeemed of the Lord can fulfill the divine requirement (Rom. 8:4).

Exodus 21

THE LAWS in this and the next two chapters are usually called "The Book of the Covenant" (24:7). They are a series of civil, social, and religious enactments which naturally follow from the promulgation of the Decalogue. They give in detail what is involved generally in our duty to God and to our neighbor. The word "judgment" probably means "decision," as though a court had pronounced. Chapter 21 deals with what are often called "the rights of persons."

Verses 2-6: The Laws Concerning Slavery. As an institution already existing, the law modified it and lessened its severities. This enactment is a striking recognition of man's essential freedom, and yet of his equally essential obligations when his choice has been made.

Verses 7-11: The right of a parent to sell his daughter was carefully guarded against abuse.

Verses 12-21: Laws Concerning Murder and Homicide. Murder was never pardoned (Gen. 9:6; Exod. 20:13), but other cases were dealt with in different ways according to circumstances. We always distinguish manslaughter and "justifiable homicide" from wilful murder. The former cases were subsequently dealt with through the cities of refuge.

Verses 15-17 are interposed as possibly likely to be connected with the cases of killing. They refer to striking parents, theft of a man ("kidnapping"), and cursing a parent.

Verses 22-25: Injuries to women who might interfere between men who quarrel, are provided against and the general law of retaliation laid down. But pecuniary compensation soon took the place of this law, owing to the difficulties and possible injustices of it.

Verses 26, 27: Assaults on slaves were not subject to the law of retaliation, but a law of compensation was enacted for them, that of compulsory emancipation.

Verses 28-32: Injuries by cattle, involving human life, are shown to be concerned with the sanctity of the person; and therefore on the principle of Genesis 9:6, the animal is to be killed, but nothing of it eaten. If the owner knew his beast was savage, he was held responsible (v. 29).

Verses 33-36: Laws concerning the rights of property, with special reference to animals.

THE MESSAGE FOR MEDITATION

(1) The sanctity of human life. (2) The freedom of human life (v. 5). (3) The reverence for parental life (20:12). (4) The Christian law of life (Matt. 5:38-42).

Exodus 22

THE LAWS ABOUT the "rights of property" are continued.
Verses 1-4: Theft.
Verses 5, 6: Trespass.
Verses 7-13: Deposits.
Verses 14, 15: Borrowing.

Verses 16-31: Various laws. There does not seem to be any order or sequence in this section. The sins are flagrant, and are, therefore, severely dealt with. The law against witchcraft

(v. 18) indicates the solemn fact of association with evil powers against God (Lev. 19:31) The law about lending (vv. 25 27), was probably due to the danger of excessive and exorbitant demands, and so it was forbidden altogether to lend on interest to their own people (Deut. 23:20; 15:7; Lev. 25:35. See Job 24:9; Prov. 28:8; Ezek. 17:13; Psa. 15:5).

THE MESSAGE FOR MEDITATION

(1) The perfect discrimination of God in regard to offences, blending tenderness and severity (vv. 1-4). (2) The law of love should dominate all our life (vv. 5-15). (3) The solemnity of trusts should always be realized (vv. 7, 8). (4) The awfulness of sin as seen in the offences mentioned (vv. 16-21). (5) The care of God for the weak and helpless (vv. 21-27).

Exodus 23

Verses 1-9: Continuation of miscellaneous laws, twelve in number.

Verses 10-13: The law of the Sabbatical Year. This was unique in the world, and associated only with Israel. The two solemn commands (v. 13) confirm these requirements.

Verses 14 17: The Law of the Feasts. Three special seasons were the feast of unleavened bread, the feast of firstfruits, and the feast of harvest. They blend the agricultural, historical, and spiritual elements. The first was instituted as they left Egypt (13:3-10), and now comes a summary of the other two, amplified later as in Leviticus 23:15-21, 34-36.

Verses 18-19: The laws of the Passover and of the firstfruits are repeated, and then the Book of the Covenant closes with a striking command which is repeated in 34:26 and Deuteronomy 14:21. Various explanations are forthcoming; perhaps it is an enactment against cruelty and an emphasis on tenderness.

Verses 20-31: General instructions, promises and warnings are a fitting close to these laws. The Angel (v. 20) was not a created angel but a divine manifestation, the Second Person of the Trinity in angelic form (v. 21).

THE MESSAGE FOR MEDITATION

(1) The absolute justice of God between man and man (vv. 1-9). (2) The loving provision of God, as seen in the Sabbatical year

(vv. 10,11). (3) The wise requirement of God as shown in the festivals as seasons for worship (vv. 12-17). (4) The gracious attitude of God, as proved by His provision, protection and promises (vv. 20-33). (5) The earnest call of God to his people to "be circumspect" (v. 13); "beware" (v. 21); "obey" (v.22). See also verses 24, 25, 32, 33.

Exodus 24

Verses 1-8: The divine recognition of the Book of the Covenant and its ratification by the people. The book (v. 7) is doubtless the germ of the Old Testament. The nearness of Moses to God, and the distance of the people, are again emphasized. The blood is very prominent (Heb. 9:19). It always means the surrender of life to God, first as propitiation, and then as consecration.

Verses 9-11: The Vision of God and the Sacrificial Feast. It is impossible to say what is meant by "they saw God." It was some appearance of the divine presence (Num. 12:8; Isa. 6:1; Ezek. 1:26).

Verses 12-18: Moses' Fellowship with God. For the purpose of receiving instructions about the Tabernacle and worship, Moses was called up to meet God. Joshua accompanied Moses for a distance and there waited six days (a solemn reminder of God's unapproachableness), when Moses was called higher to a personal and private interview with God, which lasted nearly six weeks (Deut. 9:9).

THE MESSAGE FOR MEDITATION

(1) Obedience to God (v. 3) is rendered possible only on the basis of sacrifice (vv. 5-8). (2) Reverence for God is the truest mark of discipleship. (3) Fellowship with God is the highest possible privilege.

Exodus 25

FROM CHAPTERS 25 to 31 come the divine instructions concerning the Tabernacle. The greatest necessity for the people was their continuance in the divine will and way, and this was possible only by regular worship, which would at once remind them of God and keep them in touch with Him (25:8).

Verses 1-9: Gifts for the Tabernacle were invited, and the structure was to be made strictly according to the pattern shown to Moses by God.

Verses 10-22: The Ark. The most important feature is described first of all, because it was the symbol of the approach to God. The "testimony" was the Decalogue on the tables of stone (Deut. 31:26, 27). The "mercy seat" was the place of the "covering" or forgiveness of sin (Heb. 9:5), the place of propitiation. (No one knows anything of the form or meaning of the cherubim.) See Unger's Bible Handbook pp. 44, 99.

Verses 23-30: The Shewbread. The Hebrew is "the bread of the face" or "presence," meaning that the loaves were exhibited to God (v. 30).

Verses 31-40: The Golden Lampstand. Not candlestick, because candles were unknown at that time.

THE MESSAGE FOR MEDITATION

(1) The supreme object of God is to dwell among men (John 1:18; 2 Cor. 6:16; Eph. 2:22; Rev. 21:3). (2) The only way to God is through propitiation (Rom. 3:25; Heb. 9:8-12). (3) The meeting of the soul with God is the greatest blessing in life (v. 22). (4) The ark, the shewbread, and the lampstand are full of Christ, as the propitiation, the sustenance, and the illumination of His people.

Exodus 26

AFTER THE INSTRUCTIONS as to the furniture (except the altar of incense, 30:1-10), come the details needed for the Tabernacle itself.

Verses 1-16: The Inside Curtains of Linen.

Verses 7-13: The Outer Covering of Goatskin.

Verse 14: The Outside Covering of Rams' Skins.

Verses 15-25: The Boards and Sockets.

Verses 26-30: For stability, bars were necessary to keep the boards in their places.

Verses 31-35: The Inner Veil, separating the Holy from the Most Holy place.

Verses 36, 37: The Outer Veil at the entrance to the Tabernacle.

THE MESSAGE FOR MEDITATION

Let us ponder the spiritual meaning and message of these instructions. (1) The presence of God among His people in the fact of the Tabernacle. (2) The separation of God from us because of sin, as seen in the various divisions. (3) The emphasis laid on the best possible materials as indicating God's holiness and our duty to give Him our utmost.

Exodus 27

Verses 1-8: The Brazen Altar outside the Tabernacle.

Verses 9-18: The Court in front of the Tabernacle — an oblong area, probably three hundred feet long and seventy-five broad, enclosed by curtains hung on pillars.

Verse 19: The Vessels.

Verses 20, 21: The Oil, for "Testimony" (see 25:22; 26:33).

THE MESSAGE FOR MEDITATION

(1) The altar meant sacrifice, as the one and only condition of approach. (2) The court suggested the limitations of a sacred enclosure intended only for worshippers. The space outside this court was free to all. It was called by the Romans, "pro-fanum" — "before the fane" or temple — and was a place of general concourse. Esau called "profane" in this sense (Heb. 12:16), meaning "secular," for he had no sacred enclosure in his life. (3) The oil symbolizes the Holy Spirit (John 3:34; Acts 10:38; Heb. 1:9).

Exodus 28

AFTER THE TABERNACLE comes the priesthood, by which the services were to be performed. This chapter is entirely concerned with the dress of the priest.

Verses 1-5: Appointments, and general directions as to attire.

Verses 6-12: The Ephod. A sort of vest to carry the breastplate.

Verses 13-30: The Breastplate. The exact purpose of Urim and Thummim is unknown. The words mean "Lights and Perfections," and it was used to ascertain God's will on special occasions (Num. 27:21; Deut. 33:8; 1 Sam. 28:6; Ezra 2:63), but how employed for this purpose is a matter of dispute.

Verses 31-35: The Robe under the Ephod.

Verses 36-38: The Crown or Mitre.

Verses 39-43: The Outer Garments.

THE MESSAGE FOR MEDITATION

(1) What is a priest? One who represents man to God ("unto Me" v. 3; Heb. 5:1). A prophet is one who represents God to

man (Exod. 7:1). So Christ is our representative before God (Heb. 5:1-10; 9:24). (2) The attire as here described in detail suggests God's special concern that everything in our approach to Him shall be perfect. The garments were "for glory and beauty" (v. 2). (3) The constant and profound emphasis on holiness (v. 36), shows the fundamental necessity in our approach to God. (4) The assurance given that the people were never out of God's thoughts (vv. 29, 30). In all this we can see the glory, power, comfort and inspiration of the priesthood of Christ, as the Epistle to the Hebrews shows (Heb. 4:14 to 10:25).

Exodus 29

THE CONSECRATION of the Priests.

Verses 1-4: The Offerings and the Washing.

Verses 5-9: The Investiture of Aaron and his Sons.

Verses 10-25: The Offerings.

Verses 26-34: The Priests' Portions for Food.

Verses 35-37: The Consecration repeated each day for a week, expressive of completeness (Josh. 6:3, 4; 2 Kings 5:14).

Verses 38-42: The Continual Burnt-Offering.

Verses 43-46: The Divine Assurances.

THE MESSAGE FOR MEDITATION

(1) The consecration of the priest meant entire dedication and devotion to his office. (2) The offerings emphasized redemption as the basis and well-spring of service (v. 14). (3) The washings indicated purity as the necessary preliminary and continuous accompaniment of work for God (Isa. 52:11). (4) The continual burnt-offering meant constant consecration (Rom. 12:1). (5) The meeting of the believer and God in this continual consecration (v. 42), and the consequent blessings (vv. 43-46).

Exodus 30

Verses 1-10: The Altar of Incense. The only remaining article of furniture to be described (25:10-40). Compare the smaller size of this altar with the brazen altar. Its location was in the Holy place.

Verses 11-16: The Ransom-Money. Why is this put here? Is it to provide for the great cost of the Tabernacle worship? It is also called atonement-money.

Verses 17-21: The Laver. Priests needed to be prepared for service.

Verses 22-33: The Oil. Full directions and warnings are given for its preparation and use.

Verses 34-38: The Incense. Detailed instructions about its preparation.

THE MESSAGE FOR MEDITATION

The chapter is full of spiritual symbolism and suggestion. (1) Incense means prayer (Psa. 141:2; Rev. 8:3). (2) The ransom means the gifts of redeemed sinners, as a perpetual reminder. (3) The laver means cleansing, as a pre-requisite of acceptable worship and genuine work. (4) The oil means the anointing of the Spirit, for power and blessing.

Exodus 31

Verses 1-11: The Workmen of the Tabernacle. This naturally follows the directions given. Two men are named, and they are indicated as having received divine equipment.

Verses 12-17: The Sabbath Emphasized as a Divine Sign. It is not merely a repetition of what has already been said; the references to the sign and to the penalty are new points. Perhaps these are put in here as an additional reminder of that weekly day of rest and worship, which almost more than anything else would tend to keep the people true to God.

Verse 18: The Close of the Interview between Moses and God.

THE MESSAGE FOR MEDITATION

(1) Skill of mind and hand is as much the gift of God as spiritual blessings (v. 3). (2) The use of such skill in the service of God, is both a blessing to men and a glory to God. (3) The observance of the Sabbath day is closely connected with God's consecration of the believer (v. 13). (4) The Sabbath is a sign or pledge of God's perpetual covenant with His people. The rest is for *our* refreshment (v. 17).

Exodus 32

THREE CHAPTERS now form a parenthesis, consequent on what was happening among the people in the absence of Moses. Then the instructions are resumed in chapter 35.

Verses 1-6: The Golden Calf. The impatience of the people was met by the weakness of Aaron. In verse 4, "This is thy God" is the proper translation. It was a breach of the second (not the first commandment, for it was intended to represent Jehovah (v. 5).

Verses 7-14: The Intercession of Moses. God has seen what is taking place, and proposes to destroy the people. But Moses, with three pleas, offers an effectual intercession. (1) They are God's people. (2) Egypt would be exultant. (3) The promises to the patriarchs would be unfulfilled. God's change of attitude is naturally expressed in human language.

Verses 15-20: Moses' Action. In horror, Moses broke to fragments the tables of stone. Moses is never blamed for this as sin. Was it a case of righteous indignation?

Verses 21-24: Aaron's Excuses. A revelation of deplorable weakness.

Verses 25-29: The Punishment.

Verses 30-35: Moses' Second Intercession. Note the readiness of the leader to sacrifice himself; but God would not allow it. God would spare their lives, but would punish them in His own time.

THE MESSAGE FOR MEDITATION

The sad wilfulness of those who had been wonderfully blessed of God. (2) The deplorable weakness of one who should have done better. (3) The noble willingness of a man's self-sacrifice for the sake of others (v. 32). (4) The magnificent work of intercession with God (vv. 11-13, 30-32. See Rom. 8:34; Heb. 7:25).

Exodus 33

Verses 1-6: The Divine Rebuke and Threat and their Result. Instead of God Himself, they were to have an angel, a sad loss which elicited genuine repentance.

Verses 7-11: A Temporary Tabernacle. Moses' own tent was used and its location changed (v. 7). Then God signified His approval of Moses.

Verses 12-17: The Prayer of Moses and its Answer. The threat to withdraw was revoked and gracious promises were given to Moses. The word "separated" means set apart or distinguished.

Verses 18-23: A Fresh Request. Moses evidently desired a proof of this complete restoration. He desired even a closer and fuller revelation than he had had. But he could not have the full unveiled sight of God, and so God granted him a partial revelation.

THE MESSAGE FOR MEDITATION

(1) God's concern for His own righteousness (vv. 1-6. (2) God's acknowledgment of His servant's loyalty (vv. 7-11). (3) God's answer to His servant's prayer (vv. 12-17). (4) God's condescension to His servant's desire (vv. 18-23). God's "glory" was seen in His "goodness" (vv. 18, 19).

Exodus 34

Verses 1-4: Renewal of the Tables of the Law.

Verses 5-9: The Fresh Vision of God (33:18-23). For "Jehovah" see 6:3. The elements for God's character are striking, suggesting both grace and truth. The effect on Moses was adoration and prayer.

Verses 10-17: The Covenant Renewed. Promises (vv. 10-12) are to be met by obedience (vv. 13-17).

Verses 18-26: Repetition of the instructions about the feasts, the consecration of the first-born, the Sabbath, the leaven, and the first-fruits. Once again, the legislation closes with the same command (vv. 26; 33:19).

Verses 27-35: The Closing Scenes of the Fellowship with God. The effect of this intercourse was seen in the face of Moses.

THE MESSAGE FOR MEDITATION

(1) The full revelation of the character of God (vv. 6, 7). (2) The solemn reminder of the righteousness of God (vv. 10-17). See 2 Cor. 3:18. (3) The absolute necessity of loyalty to God (vv. 18-26). (4) The blessed result of fellowship with God (vv. 29-35).

Exodus 35

Resumption of the Directions About the Tabernacle.

Verses 1-3: Before commencing work on the Tabernacle, another reminder is given of the law of the Sabbath, with a special injunction (v. 3). Why was it necessary to refer so often to the Sabbath? (16:23-30; 20:8-11; 23:12; 31:13-17). The observance was the best guarantee of continued loyalty to God.

Verses 4-20: The People and the Tabernacle. Moses tells them of the needed gifts (vv. 4-9) and work (vv. 10-19).

Verses 21-29: The Response of the People.

Verses 30-35: The Workmen Appointed.

The Message for Meditation

(1) The Sabbath is a constant reminder of "God first," and in this is the secret of abiding true to Him. (2) Giving is a real proof of true devotion to God. It is a "grace" (2 Cor. 8.7). (3) Giving should be "willing" (vv. 22, 29; 2 Cor. 8:12), and "hilarious" (Greek of 2 Cor. 9:7). (4) Giving should be proportionate and according to ability (vv. 23-29); 1 Cor. 16:2; 2 Cor. 9:7).

Exodus 36

Verses 1-3: The Commencement of the Work.

Verses 4-7: The People Restrained from Giving. The only recorded time when God's people gave too much.

Verses 8-38: The Progress of the Work. The details accord with the former instructions in chap. 26 — the inner covering (vv. 8-13); the covering above that (vv. 14-18); the outside covering (v. 19); the boards and sockets (vv. 20-30); the bars (vv. 31-34); the veil (vv. 35, 36); the curtain at the entrance (vv. 37, 38).

The Message for Meditation

(1) Superabundant giving. If only this were repeated today! (2) Splendid service. A testimony to reality. (3) Minute obedience. Everything done exactly as God had commanded.

Exodus 37

The continued Progress of the Work.

Verses 1-9: The Ark. See 25:10-20.

Verses 10-16: The Table of Shewbread (25:23-29).
Verses 17-24: The Lampstand (25:31-39).
Verses 25-29: The Incense and Oil (30:1-5). Cf. also 30:23-25, 34, 35.

THE MESSAGE FOR MEDITATION

(1) All things (not some only) are to be made according to the Divine pattern (Heb. 8:5). (2) No service is too good for God and His cause (Matt. 26:8-10). (3) The furniture of the Tabernacle as symbolical of the believer's life: the ark, the need and means of acceptance with God; the shewbread, the life presented to God, and kept ever before Him; the lampstand, the light of life to others (Matt. 5.14); the incense-altar, the need of prayer and worship, day by day.

Exodus 38

THE WORK Still in Progress.
Verses 1-7: The Brazen Altar (27:1-8).
Verse 8: The Laver (30:18).
Verses 9-20: The Court and its Gate (27:9-19).
Verses 21-31: The Sum Total of the Metal used in the Construction.

THE MESSAGE FOR MEDITATION

(1) The self-sacrifice which is based on piety (v. 8). "Motives make the man." (2) The court suggests separation, the great principle found all through the Bible (2 Cor. 6:17). (3) The vast expenditure was a testimony at once to the greatness of God's work and the liberality of God's people. (4) The exact calculation teaches the necessity of thoroughness and accuracy in all things connected with money for religious work.

Exodus 39

THE PREPARATIONS Are at Length Completed.
Verses 1-31: The Attire of the Priests.
Verses 1-7: Cf. 28:5-14.
Verses 8-21: Cf. 28:15-38.
Verses 22-26: Cf. 28:31-34.
Verses 27-29: Cf. 28:39, 40.
Verses 30, 31: Cf. 28:36, 37.

Verses 32-43: The Approval by Moses.

THE MESSAGE FOR MEDITATION

(1) The clothes were a symbol of "the beauty of holiness" (1 Chron. 16:29). (2) The exactness of obedience. Cf. "as the Lord commanded Moses" (seven times); "according to all that the Lord commanded Moses" (twice); and the closing summary, in verse 43. (3) The sole requirement of God from His children is faithfulness (not success). (See Matt. 25:21; 1 Cor. 4:2; Rev. 2:10).

Exodus 40

THE ERECTION of the Tabernacle.

Verses 1-8: Directions to Set Up the Structure and Place the Furniture. The time, a year from the Passover, would be a reminder of Egypt (12:2).

Verses 9-16: Directions as to Consecration by Anointing.

Verses 17-33: The Actual Erection.

Verses 34, 35: The Divine Recognition and Manifestation.

Verses 36-38: The Divine Guidance Indicated. The pillar of cloud (13:20-22), which had been on the temporary tabernacle (33:9), was thenceforward to be associated permanently with the Tabernacle, and by this the people would know that God was with them and what they were to do.

THE MESSAGE FOR MEDITATION

The Tabernacle was (1) the place of God's presence; (2) the place of God's worship; (3) the place where God and His people met. In all these, Christ is our Tabernacle (Greek of John 1:14). (4) The cloud was the assurance of God's presence. (5) The cloud was the sign and means of God's guidance. (6) The glory which filled the Tabernacle is promised to our lives (Psa. 84:11).

5

THE BOOK OF LEVITICUS

INTRODUCTION

I. THE TITLE

Our English title comes from the Greek, and refers to the character of the Book as "Levitical" or "priestly." The Hebrew title is taken as usual from the first words — "and he called," thereby suggesting the connection of the book with those that precede.

II. THE PURPOSE

After the covenant with Israel was established, it was essential to insure the maintenance of the relationship with God. This was done by means of worship in connection with the Tabernacle. The soul brought into fellowship with God can maintain the continuance of that fellowship only by means of regular approach to God, and this fact gives Leviticus its vital importance in the plan of Redemption. The keynote of the book is "Holiness," in its primary meaning of Separation, which includes separation *from* evil and separation *to* God. The use of Leviticus in the Epistle to the Hebrews shows its importance and spiritual meaning.[1]

III. THE CONTENTS

There are two main divisions, which, when clearly seen and remembered, help to a further and fuller analysis of the contents.

1. The way of approach to God, chapters 1 to 16. The main thought is Mediation, and all the divine instructions about offerings, priests, etc., culminate in the Day of Atonement.

2. The way of abiding with God, chapters 17 to 27. The main thought is Consecration, and all the various elements of the ritual

---

1. See the author's volume entitled *Let Us Go On — The Secret of Christian Progress in the Epistle to the Hebrews* (Zondervan Publishing House, 1944).

emphasize this thought.

Thus Israel was shown how to draw near to God, what was inconsistent with this attitude, and how, when brought near, the blessings and benefits of such a position could be maintained and manifested.

From this general outline we can proceed to a more detailed analysis, with four main divisions.

1. The Laws of the Offerings, chapters 1-7. These five offerings indicate that the *means* of approach to God is Sacrifice. The main thought is Propitiation.

2. The Laws of the Priesthood, chapters 8 to 10. This section teaches that the *instrument* of approach is Priesthood. The main thought is Mediation.

3. The Laws of Purity, chapters 11 to 22. These show that the *condition* of approach is Purity. The main thought is Separation. N.B. — Chapters 11 to 15 give the requirements in preparation for the Day of Atonement (chap. 16), and then in chapters 17 to 22 the subject is continued by showing the separated life in various aspects. This section has been usefully divided into (a) the physical man (chaps. 11 to 15); (b) the spiritual man (chaps. 16 and 17); (c) The moral man (chaps. 18 to 22).

4. The Laws of the Festivals, chapters 23 to 27. These give the *occasions* of approach, in the Festivals. The main thought is Consecration, as indicated by the theme of praise.

A general view of the whole book in these four sections has been helpfully stated thus:

(1) The Ritual of the Holy Altar: Sacrifice;
(2) The Ritual of the Holy Persons: Service;
(3) The Ritual of the Holy Place: Separation;
(4) The Ritual of the Holy Times: Sanctification.

IV.   THE CHARACTER

The legislation of the Pentateuch arises out of the history, and is constantly and closely connected with it. There are three codes of laws: (1) The Covenant Code, Exodus 20 to 24; (2) The Priests' Code, Exodus 25 to 40, and Leviticus; (3) The People's Code, Deuteronomy. Thus Leviticus is concerned with instructions for worship intended for the guidance of the priests, just as Deuteronomy is the book intended for the guidance of the people.

Leviticus is almost all legislation, the only history being in chapters 8 to 10 and 24: 10-23.

The phrase, "The Lord spake to Moses," is found at least thirty times, and no other book has this feature (1:1; 8:1; 11:1; 17:1, and subdivisions also).

For references to Leviticus in the New Testament, see Matthew 8:4; 12:4; 15:4; 19:19; 22:39; Luke 2:22; Hebrews: chaps. 9 and 10; James 2:8; 1 Peter 1:16.

V. THE MESSAGE

After Redemption (Exod. 1 to 12) and Instruction (20 to 40), comes Worship. As Exodus tells of the Tabernacle, Leviticus shows how it was to be used. "There will I meet with thee." Everything is concerned with the maintenance of the true relation to God. The keyword is Holiness (10:3). No other book has so many lessons on access to God and worship (Psa. 65:4). "Offering" and "Sacrifice" occur ninety-one times. "Holy" and its cognates 131 times. "Clean" and its cognates and contrasts 186 times. It is the only book by means of which the Epistle to the Hebrews is understood. The following truths are symbolized and emphasized in Leviticus.

1. The Great Problem: Sin.
2. The Great Provision: Sacrifice.
3. The Great Power: Priesthood.
4. The Great Plan: Day of Atonement.
5. The Great Possibility: Access to God.
6. The Great Principle: Holiness.
7: The Great Privilege: The Presence of God.

Thus the Book teaches that access to God and communion with Him are essential to life, that they are only possessed on the ground of Redemption (Exod. 5:1), and through the Sacrifice and Priesthood of Christ (Heb. 10:5-25), by which the laws of Holiness are made possible (1 Peter 1:16). God's order must always be preserved. As Leviticus follows Exodus, so communion, holiness, worship must follow (and cannot precede) pardon. "An unpardoned rebel cannot have access to the king's favor." Leviticus thus emphasizes the necessity, teaches the possibility, provides for the reality, and assures of the completeness of Holiness (2 Cor. 7:1).

CHAPTER STUDIES

Leviticus 1

IN CONSIDERING the five offerings (chaps. 1-7), it is to be noted that each has its special requirements, and these indicate the special meaning. The Burnt-offering, which comes first, was wholly consumed on the altar, and this suggests entire consecration. The offering implying consecration is put first, instead of that which meant expiation, because the offerings were for Israel as God's people, already in covenant with Him on the basis of the redemption sacrifice of the Passover. Because of this relationship, they are here shown that the Burnt-offering symbolizes the complete dedication of their lives to God. The divine source of these instructions is strikingly shown (v. 1). Offerings were already familiar ("if"), but now God was regulating them especially for Israel. The vital features of the Burnt-offering were the actual offering of the animal (vv. 3, 4), the slaying (v. 5), the offering of the blood — symbolizing the life given in death and surrender to God — and the burning (v. 9). The first two were the work of the offerer, the third that of the priest, and the fourth that of the fire, representing the action of God. For the law of the Burnt-offering, see 6:8-13.

THE MESSAGE FOR MEDITATION

The Burnt-offering may be interpreted of Christ and of Christians. (1) Christ as the Burnt-offering means His entire surrender, even to death, to do the Father's will. The word "atonement" originally meant "at-onement" or reconciliation, as in Romans 5:11 (Greek). (2) The believer as a Burnt-offering means that everything we are and have belongs to God, to be used for His glory. Romans 12:1 suggests the Burnt-offering.

Leviticus 2

THE MEAT-OFFERING (meat, meaning food in general, not flesh-meat) is better called the Meal-offering. It is one of the "unbloody" sacrifices, and the Hebrew word for it, *minchah*, means a "gift." It is used in Genesis 4:3, 4; 32:13; 43:11. The offering seems to suggest man's homage to God, as shown by the presentation of the products of the earth. The fundamental thought is that of 1 Chronicles 29:14, 16, the only idea being that of a gift pleasing to God. Three varieties are mentioned (vv. 1-3; 4-11; 14-16), indicative of different circumstances in the offerer. The man's part was to bring his gift, and the priest had to present a part of it on the brazen altar and burn it, and then to eat the rest. This last point marks a difference from the Burnt-offering, which was entirely burnt. While the Meal-offering accompanied the Burnt-offering (Num. 15:4), it was a separate offering. The Burnt-offering symbolized the life devoted to God, and the Meal-offering the fruits of labor consecrated to Him. The features are noteworthy: (1) The oil was a type of the Holy Spirit. (2) Frankincense meant that the offering was to be accomplished by prayer (Psa. 141:2). (3) The absence of leaven meant purity. (4) The absence of honey meant also the absence of everything impure or even doubtful (honey ferments and decays). (5) The salt meant preservation and permanence as indicative of God's covenant. (6) The fire meant God's entire acceptance. (7) The "sweet savor" meant God's approval of and pleasure in the offering. For the law of the Meal-offering, see 6:14-23.

THE MESSAGE FOR MEDITATION

The Meal-offering symbolizes (1) Christ as the One who realized perfectly the consecration of His life's service to God. St. Mark's Gospel illustrates Christ as the "Servant of Jehovah," and the "sweet savor" of God's approval is seen in Mark 1:11; Ephesians 5:2. (2) The Meal-offering suggests the full surrender and dedication of our work to God: —

> That all our powers with all their might,
> to Thy sole glory may unite.

See 1 Corinthians 10:31; Colossians 1:10; 1 Thessalonians 4:1.

Leviticus 3

THE PEACE-OFFERING. The distinctive feature of this offering was the feast upon the sacrifice. This indicates its meaning. The Burnt-offering meant consecration to God. The Meal-offering signified the presentation of powers and products to God in homage and service. But this offering with its feast symbolized reconciliation, as shown in the fellowship of eating. One portion of the offering was consumed by fire, indicating God's acceptance and participation. Another portion was actually eaten by the offerer, and a third was eaten by the priests. The last does not seem to have been a feature of the actual reconciliation between God and the worshipper, but as in the Meal-offering, it was the portion intended for the maintenance of the priest. Eating is always an element in a covenant, and so this participation indicated the oneness subsisting between God and the worshipper. The Peace-offering was one of those which existed before the time of Moses (Gen. 31:54; Ex. 32:6), but was given a fresh sanctification by God in communion with Israel. The offering could be from the cattle (vv. 1-5), or the sheep (vv. 6-11), or from the goats (vv. 12-15). The prohibition of the use of fat or blood for food (vv. 16, 17) is very significant (see 17:11, 12). In verse 9, "the whole rump" should be "the whole fat tail", referring to a special breed of sheep. Kellogg holds that the feast was given by God to the Israelite, not by the man to God, because the offering was already God's possession. This, therefore, is the contrast between the heathen and Scriptural idea of the feast. In one, "man feasts God"; in the other, "God feasts man." For the law of the Peace-offering, see 7:11-21.

THE MESSAGE FOR MEDITATION

The Peace-offering is to be related to Christ and to us. (1) The Lord is our Peace-offering, having made reconciliation (Col. 1:20; Eph. 2:14-17). (2) Our appropriation of Christ and participation in His sacrificial work brings peace to us (Rom. 5:1). Eating is always the symbol of reconciliation and fellowship (Luke 14:15-24; Matt. 22:1-14; Psa. 23:5; 36:8). Fellowship is the highest point of Christian privilege.

Leviticus 4

THE SIN-OFFERING. The predominant thought is the need of propitiation, expiation, atonement, in approaching God. The reason why the Burnt-offering, Meal-offering, and Peace-offering come before this in order is probably because, as these offerings were for those who were already in covenant with God on the basis of the Passover Sacrifice of Redemption, the thoughts of Consecration, Service and Fellowship are emphasized first as the immediate consequences of the position of the redeemed people.

Then comes the Sin-offering, with its message of the constant need of expiation in the life of a believer. Besides, the previous offerings were familiar before, and were incorporated into Israel's religion; but the Sin-offering was an entirely new institution. All these sacrifices are those of God's people, not of the unconverted sinner. They tell how the believer's life is to be lived. The requirements for the Sin-offering differed, and were graded according to the positions occupied: priest (vv. 2-12), or the entire people (vv. 13-21), or ruler (vv. 22-26), or ordinary person (vv. 27-35). The elaborate instructions would teach very impressively the awful reality of sin. The phrase "through ignorance" means inadvertently, and shows that even for such wrongdoing a sacrifice is necessary. God's righteousness cannot overlook any sin, but His love provides a sacrifice for inadvertent wrong-doing.

THE MESSAGE FOR MEDITATION

(1) The Sin-offering is pre-eminently a type of Christ as our propitiation and expiation. See also Isaiah 53; Matthew 26:28; 1 Peter 2:24. As such, He is our substitute, "the just for the unjust." (2) The result to us is that our sin is removed, cancelled, because of His death "for," that is "instead of" us. Sin is forgiven because the innocent Victim has offered a Sacrifice of expiation. (For the law of the Sin-offering, see 6:25-30).

Leviticus 5

Verses 1-13 are probably, indeed almost certainly, to be interpreted of the Sin-offering, continued from the previous chapter (see A.S.V. margin of v. 6), and especially because of the references to the Sin-offering in verses 6, 7, and 9. This section deals with the Sin-offering required from ordinary people, according to the capacity of the offerer. It is important to notice that, notwithstanding points of contact with the requirements of the other offerings, this Sin-offering is made prominent by its emphasis on expiation. In particular, great stress is laid on the sprinkling of blood (4:6, 7, 16-18, 25, 30; 5:9), which is also so prominent in the New Testament (Rom. 5:9; 1 Pet. 1:2; Heb. 12:24; 1 John 1:7). The eating and burning of the Sin-offering "without the camp" should also be noted, and its typical meaning carefully pondered (Heb. 13:10-12).

Verses 13-19: The Trespass-offering. Another new require-ment for Israel. The difference between this and the Sin-offering is that, in the Sin-offering, the main thought is that of *guilt,* while in the Trespass-offering it is *injury* done to God and man. The one emphasizes *expiation* and the latter *satisfaction.* By this means the sinner will be reinstated in the covenant with God. The ritual accordingly differs from that of the Sin-offering, and seems to suggest the thought of reparation. In these verses the sin concerns "the holy things of the Lord." Notice again the emphasis on ignorance and the need of sacrifice (vv. 17, 18, 19).

THE MESSAGE FOR MEDITATION

(1) Christ as our Trespass-offering means that God's rights must be upheld because sin is an offence against His position and character, and calls for reparation. The thought of *satisfaction* is a very important aspect of Christ's atoning work. (2) Our recognition of this truth will lead to the consciousness that *reparation* is due from us, and that Christ has made it on our behalf.

Leviticus 6

Verses 1-7: Continuation of the laws of the Sin-offering, with special reference to wrongs against man, as 5:14-19 dealt with wrongs against God. Five cases are mentioned, and, in each, restitution is required. Confession and reparation must be made to the one wronged and an offering presented to God.

Verses 8-13: The Law of the Burnt-offering for the Guidance of the Priests. See 1:1-17. The priests are instructed to offer this Burnt-offering continually.

Verses 14-23: The Law of the Meal-offering. See 2:1-16. Like the Burnt-offering, the Meal-offering was to be "perpetual."

Verses 24-30: The Law of the Sin-offering. See 4:1-35. The priests are taught the special solemnity and sanctity of the Sin-offering.

THE MESSAGE FOR MEDITATION

(1) Sins against man need to be met by confession and restitu-tion. (2) Christ as the Burnt-offering suggests continual conse-cration, but, as the Sin-offering, His work is done "once for all" (Heb. 9:12). So we are to be continually consecrated to God, a Burnt-offering always offered to His praise. (3) Priestly life

and service cannot be too particular in its care for the will of God to be done at every point. The best proof of life is faithfulness in little things.

Leviticus 7

Verses 1-10: The Law of the Trespass-offering. See 5:14 to 6:7.

Verses 11-34: The law of the Peace-offering. See 3:1-17. Scofield suggests that the reason this is removed from its place as the third offering, and put last here, is that the Peace-offering symbolizes the first need of the sinner, reconciliation, and that thus experience called for the placing of the Peace-offering in the order of 3:-1-17. Why is leaven to be offered (v. 13) after "unleavened wafers" are mentioned (v. 12)? Is it that verse 12 is a type of Christ (sinless) and verse 13 refers to us as sinful, notwithstanding our relation to God?

Verses 35-38: Concluding summary as to the offerings, with special reference to the priests' portions and duties. These detailed instructions emphasize the fact and meaning of sin.

The Message for Meditation

The instructions to the priests (6:8 to 7:38), as distinct from those to the people, and especially the assignment of portions to the priests (6:16-18, 26; 7:6-10, 14, 31-36), are very significant. They indicate (1) God's care for His servants (1 Cor. 9:13, 14). (2) The"Heave-offering" (raised toward heaven) suggests recognition of the God of heaven and dependence on Him. (3) The "Wave-offering" (moved from left to right) was probably an acknowledgment of God as among His people, the God of Redemption. Thus, we have in these two offerings "God the Infinitely High" and "God the Infinitely Nigh." The priests were thereby continually reminded of God and their close relation to Him.

Leviticus 8

The second part of the Book commences here (see outline). After the sacrifices come the divine requirements for the priests who are to offer them. This section (chaps. 8-10) is, with a slight exception (chap. 24), the only historical part of Leviticus. Originally, the head of the family was the priest. Then came the consecration of the first-born for this purpose (Exod. 13). Later, the Levites were to take the place of the first-born (Num. 3:13, 41-45), and out of this tribe one family. Aaron's was selected. But when the family grew to large proportions David arranged it in twenty-four courses. The record here should be compared with Exodus 28 and 29. After the preliminaries (vv. 1-5), four main features of the consecration are seen: cleansing (vv. 6, 13; clothing (vv. 7-9); anointing (vv. 10-12); and sacrificing (vv. 14-22). Great stress is laid on all this being from God, not man (vv. 1, 4, 5, 9, 13, 17, 21, 29, 34-36). Every detail was in some way symbolical.

In *verses* 23-26, the application of the blood to ear, hand, and foot, suggests the consecration of these faculties to God.

In *verse* 30, the blood and the oil (symbols of Calvary and Pentecost) are applied.

Verses 31, 32 order a feast, and *verses* 33-36 command a repetition of these ceremonies each day during seven days, thereby emphasizing their value and importance. The chapter indicates the two qualifications for priesthood mentioned in Hebrews 5:1-4, oneness with man (vv. 1-3) and authority from God (v. 4). Moses had to perform the consecration ceremonies, thereby showing him as exercising priestly duties for the last time.

THE MESSAGE FOR MEDITATION

(1) Christ is our Priest (Heb. 5:9, 10), representing us to God (Heb. 5:1), fulfilling the two requirements of authority from God (Heb. 5:5, 6) and oneness with man (Heb. 5:7, 8). His Priesthood is emphasized in Hebrews as the safeguard against the believer sinning (Heb. 4:14-16; 7:25). (2) All believers are priests, having direct access to God (1 Pet. 2:5; Rev. 1:6). The four requirements for the consecration of the Aaronic Priesthood — sacrifice, washing, clothing and anointing — symbolize respectively our need of acceptance, cleansing, justification and sanctification, while the seven days of separation (vv. 33-35) indicate our entire dedication to the work of the Christian priesthood.

Leviticus 9

THE WORK of the Priests Begun.

Verses 1-7: After the seven days of consecration, Aaron and his sons commenced their priestly work. They were instructed as to offerings for themselves and the people.

Verses 8-14: The offerings for the priests. Even for them atonement was necessary before they could render acceptable service.

Verses 15-21: The offerings for the people. Thus, on the foundation of sacrifice and by means of the mediating priesthood, the nation could now approach God in the Tabernacle. The order of the offerings should be compared with that of chapters 1 to 7. This is the order of experience: Sin-offering; Burnt-offering; Meal-offering; Peace-offering.

Verse 22: Aaron finished his work of offering by returning and blessing the people. Numbers 6:24-27 gives the full form.

Verse 23: The commission of Aaron in connection with the Tabernacle, and then the second benediction, Moses being associated in it.

Verses 23-24: The divine recognition and confirmation of all these ceremonies. "Glory" means the "manifestation of splendor" and God's revelation of Himself was doubtless by means of the Shekinah or cloud over the Tabernacle. The fire meant acceptance and approval after obedience, and the people's attitude was one of awe.

THE MESSAGE FOR MEDITATION

The chapter has three main thoughts: (1) Sacrifice from the people to God (atonement first, then consecration, then fellowship). (2) Blessing for the people from God (benediction and benefaction). (3) Testimony to the people from God (obedience followed by assurance — "Them that honor Me I will honor").

Leviticus 10

Verses 1-7: The Sin of Nadab and Abihu. It was still the first day of the new priesthood's work (chap. 9), and these two sons of Aaron did something which is called offering "strange fire." Perhaps they lit their censers from an ordinary fire, instead of from the fire on the altar of Burnt-offering (6:12; 16:12). Or they offered the incense in some way in which God had not commanded. Whatever it was, it is called "strange fire" and the summary judgment of God descended. It was necessary to show at the outset the real character of God (v. 3; cf. Acts 5:1). Aaron and his sons were to remain in the Tabernacle as consecrated men, and not to show to the people the marks of personal sorrow in the face of this righteous judgment (v. 6). Their relatives were to remove and bury the bodies. The principle is the same as in Matthew 8:21, 22.

Verses 8-11: The context seems to indicate that Nadab and Abihu had done this wrong under the excitement of semi-intoxication, which prevented them from distinguishing between the right and the wrong way of serving God (v. 10).

Verses 12-20: Moses took all possible care that the rest of that day's service should be according to God's will (vv. 12-15): but there was one point still in error (vv. 16-18). The blood should have been presented and the flesh burned (9:15); but the former had not been done, while the latter had. Aaron replied to the expostulation of Moses by pointing out the exceptional circumstances of that day: "Could it be the will of God that a house in which was found the guilt of such a sin should yet partake of the most holy things of God in the sanctuary?" (*Kellogg*). This seems a more likely explanation than the one sometimes given that Aaron was too distressed to be fit to eat the Sin-offering. Moses accepted the explanation, whatever it was. The spirit of the law had been observed, even if the letter had been broken (Hos. 6:8; Matt. 12:7).

THE MESSAGE FOR MEDITATION

(1) The peril of the sin of presumption. God's orders, not our own ideas are to be followed at any cost (1 Sam. 15:22; Col. 2:23). (2) Spiritual worship cannot be furthered by carnal or mere human means (Phil. 3:9, A.S.V.). (3) The danger of excitement in religion. The contrast between the spirit of alcohol and the Holy Spirit is found very significantly (Luke 1:15; Eph. 5:13). But excitement takes various forms. It is easy to mistake physical excitement for the work of the Spirit. The need of balance for spiritual discernment is essential (v. 10). (4) No one, however great, is immune from God's judgments. God's character (v. 3) has not been modified by the freedom of the Gospel (Heb. 10:31; 12:29). While we have "entrance," it is still into the "holiest" (Heb. 10:19).

Leviticus 11

THE THIRD PART of the Book commences here. After the offerings and the priesthood follow the natural consideration of that impurity which keeps man from God. This is both ceremonial and moral. Chapters 11 to 15 deal with bodily uncleanness, and the first aspect is the question of food. It is not always easy to see the reason for the prohibitions, but it would seem that the primary principle was sanitary, and one proof of this is the greater immunity from ill-health and disease found among the Jews. This in turn suggests a moral basis in the antithesis of death and life, for "whatever tends to weakness or disease by that fact tends to death" (*Kellogg*). Thus, the prohibitions are usually associated with foulness of appearance or uncleanness of habits, and these are thought of as symbolical of sin.

Verses 2-8: Regulations about quadrupeds. The prohibition refers to animals which either part the hoof or chew the cud, or do both.

Verses 9-12: Fish. Permission is limited to those that have fins and scales.

Verses 13-19: Birds. No marks are given, but the prohibition covers carnivorous birds and those of unclean habits.

Verses 20-23: Insects. Those that leap are permitted, those that run are forbidden.

Verses 24-28: Rules about contact with death.

Verses 29-30: Creeping things.

Verses 31-40: Further reference to contact with death.

Verses 41-43: Vermin.

Verses 44-47: The great principle, holiness, which underlies these laws.

The Message for Meditation

(1) The supreme necessity of holiness (vv. 44-47). God takes every possible way of emphasizing this truth. (2) The Gospel for the body. "Glorify God in your body" (1 Cor. 6:20); "present your bodies" (Rom. 12:1); "eat or drink . . . to the glory of God" (1 Cor. 10:31). The New Testament lays great stress on the body as a part of our redeemed being. See 1 Thessalonians 5:23; 1 Corinthians 6:13-19.

Leviticus 12

THE SECOND ASPECT of bodily or ceremonial uncleanness is that of childbirth. This is a natural sequence of the reference to the body in chapter 11.

Verses 2, 4, 5: The laws of purification. The impurity is ceremonial, not moral, physical conditions being regarded (as in chapter 11) as symbolical of sin.

Verse 3: The law of circumcision. This is from Genesis 17:12, and doubtless includes physical purity and moral purity. (See Lev. 26:41; Col. 2:10, 11; Phil. 3:3).

Verses 6-8: The law of the offerings. Compare Luke 2:22-24.

THE MESSAGE FOR MEDITATION

(1) Every phase of life is to be holy unto the Lord. (2) The deepest and most sacred elements of home-life are always to be related to God. (3) Holiness involves atonement (v. 7) and purification.

Leviticus 13

THE THIRD INSTANCE of bodily uncleanness, Leprosy. This is especially mentioned because of the offensiveness of the appearance and the seriousness of the actual condition. There are several forms of leprosy, as well as other skin diseases. This is usually regarded as that which is known to the medical profession as elephantiasis. The first indication is a spot in the flesh which develops into an ulcer, which may continue without apparent progress for a long time, but at last it proceeds to the stages of disfigurement and disease, followed, when it reaches a vital part, by death. While sanitary conditions are, as before, included in these regulations, the moral element is particularly prominent, as will be seen from the requirement of the priest (v. 2) rather than the doctor. Leprosy was in several respects a very definite type of sin.

Verses 1-8: The question of doubtful cases.

Verses 9-11: Actual cases.

Verses 12-17: Real and apparent cases.

Verses 18-39: Various methods of testing.

Verses 40-44: Leprosy on the head.

Verses 45, 46: Treatment of the leper.

Verses 47-59: Leprosy in the clothes. For Bible instances of lepers, see Numbers 12:12; 2 Kings 5:1-27; Matthew 8:1-4; Luke 17:11-19.

THE MESSAGE FOR MEDITATION

(1) Leprosy as a type of sin: insignificant and painless at the outset; gradual though slow development; serious results to the person; repulsiveness to others; incurable by human means; the issue, death. (2) Leprosy as causing separation (from man and the congregation). See Isaiah 59:2. (3) Leprosy as dealt with by the priest, who had to (a) examine; (b) declare; (c) insist on the requirements being fulfilled. So Christ our Priest tests, pronounces and commands. But the priest could not cure, Christ can. See next chapter.

Leviticus 14

THE CLEANSING of the Leper.

The elaborate details of the purification are very striking. They show the mind of God for Israel in the matter of cleansing and its symbolical meaning.

Verses 1-8: The first stage of the purification. This restored the leper, under certain conditions, to the camp of Israel and to association with others. The four features are all apparently symbolical of spiritual realities: the sprinkling of the blood; the cedar wood (antiseptic properties; scarlet color of blood); hyssop (perhaps possessing healing qualities). The two birds represent (as elsewhere) the double type (one alone being insufficient) of death and resurrection. There are several illustrations of this truth, e.g., the double leadership of Moses and Joshua; the two goats of chap. 16. It is important to observe that the priest, not the physician, is mentioned, and yet even the priest could not cure (God alone could do that), but only declare clean and see that the proper requirements were fulfilled.

Verses 9-32: The second stage of the purification, restoring the leper to his home. All these ceremonies would give assurance to the man, and make his reinstatement a genuine satisfaction.

Verses 33-53: The cleansing of the house. A further indication of the fact, peril, and consequences of leprosy. The "eighth day" (v. 10) is symbolical of resurrection, "the morrow after the sabbath."

THE MESSAGE FOR MEDITATION

(1) The cleansing of the leper typifies the work of Christ for us. (a) The leper could do nothing for his own cleansing

and cure. (b) The sacrifice points to the Blood of Christ (Heb. 9:22). (c) The priest was God's representative, in regard to the requirements for the assurance of cleansing and to the re-instatement (see Heb. 4:14-16; 10:19-25). (d) The resurrection following the sacrifice was the proof to all that every obstacle had been removed (Rom. 4:25). (2) The cleansing of the home sug-gests the need of a pure environment if we are to live aright. True social life, true family life, true church life, must be, and will be, the outcome of personal cleansing and consecration.

Leviticus 15

THE FOURTH CAUSE of ceremonial impurity due to physical defilement.

There are five cases mentioned:

Verses 2-15; 16, 17, 18; 19-24; 25-30. Or the questions can be considered in reference to men (vv. 2-18) and to women (vv. 19-30). The repulsiveness implied is at once a physical peril and a moral parable (v. 31).

THE MESSAGE FOR MEDITATION

(1) The solemn emphasis on sin. The chapter suggests sin as ingrained in the nature, and as such, going far deeper than any act of the will. There is a real distinction between sin and sins, between root and fruit, between nature and practice. There is, therefore, a clear difference between unconscious and conscious sins. The former are suggested and symbolized by this chapter, and need atonement and cleansing equally with those of which we are conscious. (2) The special emphasis on cleansing. Scripture is full of this truth. The cleansing power of the Blood of Christ for expiation and the cleansing power of the Word and Spirit for purification (Psa. 19:12; John 13:3-10; Eph. 5:25-27; 1 John 1:9). This is the "double cure" covering the removal of guilt and the provision of purity.

Leviticus 16

THE ANNUAL Day of Atonement was the center and culmination of the Hebrew festivals. Every observance led up to this. "What the fifty-third of Isaiah is to the Messianic prophecies, that the sixteenth of Leviticus is to the whole system of Mosaic types —

the most consummate flower of the Messianic symbolism" (*Kellogg*). It was the occasion for the ceremonial purification of the entire congregation. The defilement of the camp as a whole needed this annual ceremony, with its outstanding emphasis on the Sin-offering.

Chronologically it comes after chapter 10 (see v. 1). The key-word is Atonement (v. 33) and includes atonement for Aaron and his house (v. 6), for the Tabernacle (vv. 15, 17), for the brazen altar (vv. 18, 19), and for the congregation (vv. 20-22, 33).

Amid the details of the chapter, the main features of the day were four: (1) The sacrifices on the brazen altar; (2) The entrance of the High Priest through the Holy Place into the Holy of Holies. This was the only occasion of entrance, and it was always by the High Priest alone; (3) The sprinkling of the blood on and around the Mercy Seat in the Holy of Holies; (4) The return of the High Priest after the performance of his duties.

Part of the sacrificial work under section (1) above, was the ceremonial of the two goats "one for Jehovah, and one for the scapegoat" (v. 8). The word translated "scapegoat" is *Azazel* (see A.S.V.), and this has led to differences of opinion as to the meaning and purpose. Only two views need be mentioned. (1) Some think that *Azazel* means an evil spirit. But there are serious, perhaps insuperable, objections to this view. Not only is the term not found elsewhere, but it is impossible to think of the Sin-offering being divided between Jehovah and Satan. And the idea of appeasing an evil spirit with an offering is unthinkable. The only possibility in this view is that of the goat for *Azazel* meaning a symbolical announcement to Satan that expiation by sacrifice has destrc ed his power over the forgiven sinner (*Kellogg*). This word expresses the truth of Revelation 12:10, 11. (2) The other and truer view is that the two goats (like the two birds of chap. 14) symbolize the two aspects of the Atonement, namely, the expiation and removal (see A.S.V. marg.) of sin, as suggested by Christ's Death and Resurrection (Rom. 4:25). No single type is complete in itself, and hence the need of two goats to express the full truth (see Psa. 103:12; Micah 7:19).

THE MESSAGE FOR MEDITATION

(1) The High Priest, a type of Christ. The spiritual meaning of Leviticus 16 is seen in Hebrews 9, and the four parts named above correspond to Christ's Death, Ascension, Life in Heaven, Second Coming — or what may be described as His Atonement, Approach, Appeal, and Advent (see Heb. 9:24-28). (2) The supreme purpose of God for man is fellowship, unhindered by sin. And the way of approach is through sacrifice (Heb. 9: 8, 11, 24; 10:19, 20).

Leviticus 17

AFTER INSTRUCTIONS about Sacrifices (chaps. 1 to 7), Priesthood (chaps. 8 to 10), Purifications (chaps. 11 to 15), and the Day of Atonement (chap. 16), it is natural and fitting that emphasis should be laid on the place where all these were to be observed. The people were not to think that any place would do — there was only one, the place of God's appointment (Deut. 16:5, 6). Some writers hold that this chapter is not so much concerned with the place of sacrifice as with the fact that all slaying, even for ordinary food, should be associated with the Tabernacle, and regarded as something sacred. It is urged that such ordinary slaughter at the Tabernacle was possible while the Israelites were together in the wilderness, but that it was naturally abrogated as impossible when they were settled in Canaan (Deut. 12:15-24). This would, therefore, teach the need of associating sacredness with even their common food and of observing "holiness in eating" (*Kellogg*). But it seems in every way simpler and better to regard the chapter in the former light mentioned above, as teaching the duty of regarding one place as that alone in which all worship was to be observed.

Verses 2-9: The one place for all worship. The old priesthood of the patriarchal family was now superseded by the Aaronic line, and the ordinary places of worship at home were set aside for the Tabernacle. The "devils" (v. 7) are "he-goats" or "hairy ones" (Deut. 32:17; 2 Chron. 11:15), a form of Egyptian idolatry to which Israel was probably very prone.

Verses 10-16: The prohibition in regard to blood (see Gen. 9:4; Lev. 3:17; 7:26; 19:26; Deut. 12:16; 15:23). While the basis of the prohibition was doubtless hygienic, as modern science now proves, the prominent reason was religious, suggesting the sacredness of the means of sacrifice.

THE MESSAGE FOR MEDITATION

(1) The one place suggests Christ as the one and only Way (John 14:6; Acts 4:12). (2) The command as to blood is in striking contrast to John 6:53, 54; Matthew 26, 27, 28. We appropriate the atonement for salvation. (3) If the chapter refers to "holiness in eating," we see the principle of 1 Corinthians 10:31, and the meaning of "grace before meat."

Leviticus 18

HITHERTO, the divine injunctions have had to do with physical uncleanness; now follows, naturally, God's commands against various forms of moral impurity. This is the theme of chapters 18 to 20, which form a distinct section.

Verses 1-5: Introduction to the Hebrew Law of Marriage (see Exod. 3:15; 6:2-4; 19:1-6).

Verses 6-18: Details of the Law. Restraints to guard against sin. "Near of kin" (v. 6) is the key-thought of the whole, and affinity and consanguinity are regarded as the same. The breaches of the law here mentioned were common in Egypt and Canaan. The law of v. 16 was set aside for a special purpose in Deuteronomy 25:5.

Verses 19-23: Further Prohibitions: v. 21 is put here because idolatry and licentiousness were invariably associated.

Verses 24-30: Solemn Warnings. The relation of national life to individual life is emphasized. "Dissolute morals are always a symptom which precedes the ruin of an empire, or the fall of a nation" (*Meyrick*).

THE MESSAGE FOR MEDITATION

Holiness is best realized in connection with the nature and character of God. (1) The Basis of Holiness (vv. 2-4) — "I am the Lord your God." God's character and His claim on us form the foundation of true life. (2) The Principle (v. 3) : — separation from surrounding life. Unlikeness to others based on likeness to God. (3) The Evidence (vv. 4, 5) : — obedience in heart and life, character and conduct.

Leviticus 19

FURTHER LAWS on Holiness. This chapter is an extension
of chapter 18. From licentiousness, the laws proceed to deal
with other kinds of unfaithfulness to God and man. There does
not seem to be any system in the presentation, but v. 2 is, perhaps, a sort of binding principle for all. The various duties are
all associated with the great truth of God's holiness. This
chapter has been well called "the Old Testament counterpart of
the Sermon on the Mount, inasmuch as it lays down the law of
conduct as the latter lays down the principle of action."

Verses 1-8: Special emphasis on two great principles of honor
to parents and reverence to God. Through the former we learn
the latter, as in our earliest days our parents are God's representatives. Our duty to God is seen here in relation to the
Sabbath (v. 3), the avoidance of idolatry (v. 4), and the proper
observance of the Peace-offering (vv. 5-8).

Verses 9-18: Five duties of man to man (two verses to each).

Verses 19-32: Various regulations, all based on obedience
in general (v. 19), and associated with true devotion and conduct as opposed to idolatry and unfaithfulness.

THE MESSAGE FOR MEDITATION

(1) The Meaning of Holiness. The primary and fundamental
idea is *separateness*. In God this implies His transcendence,
His remoteness from everything earthly and wrong. In us it
means separation in the sense of consecration to God. This
thought of separateness is the basic truth wherever holiness is
found in Scripture. Then follows a natural and necessary con-
sequence, that the separateness in God indicates His unique
character, while in us it means purity of heart and life. (2) The
emphasis on "I am the Lord" and "I am the Lord your God"
(found fifteen times) suggests that the primary reason for all
holiness and obedience is the character and authority of God
(v. 2). See 1 Peter 1:15, 16.

Leviticus 20

THE SUBJECT of chapter 18 is here resumed by attaching
penalties to the commission of the sins. Wrongs are often done

against man as well as God. Sin is evil in relation to God, and crime is evil in relation to man.

Verses 1-6: The first part of the code, with special reference to the sin of sacrificing to Molech.

Verses 7, 8: The foundation reason for all these laws.

Verses 9-21: The second part of the code.

Verses 22-26: General conclusion.

Verse 27: (see v. 6). The various penalties should be noted, (1) stoning vv. 2, 27; (2) death (method not described); (3) excommunication (divine and human) vv. 4-6, 17, 18; (4) burning (that is, after having been first put to death, Josh. 7:25), v. 14; (5) bearing iniquity (without being accepted through sacrifice) vv. 17, 19, 20; (6) childlessness (the children dying first, or else they are not to be reckoned as belonging to the father) vv. 20, 21.

The Message for Meditation

The severity shows God's view of the heinousness of evil. (1) The two sins: defiling and profaning (v. 3). (2) The two requirements: sanctification, obedience (vv. 7, 8). (3) The two reasons: difference from other nations (vv. 23, 24), ownership by God (v. 26).

Leviticus 21

Chapters 21 and 22 form a section dealing with defilements and defects of the priests. Beyond and above the requirements of God for the people, there were special regulations for the priests, including references to ceremonial and moral defilements and physical defects.

Verses 1-6: Ceremonial defilements due to family relations, with verse 6 as the chief reason for the divine order.

Verses 7-9: Moral defilements.

Verses 10-15: Special emphasis on the High Priest with respect to defilement. Not even his private sorrows were to interfere with his public work.

Verses 16-24: Disqualification through physical defects.

The Message for Meditation

(1) The supreme importance of reality and purity in those who are called to special service for God. Not that there are

two standards of holiness, but the priests were to show (as Christian workers should today) what God really meant for all. "Be ye clean, that bear the vessels of the Lord" (Isa. 52:11); "That the ministry be not blamed" (2 Cor. 6:3). (2) The necessity of keeping in mind the fundamental idea of holiness as a setting-apart for the service of God (v. 8).

Leviticus 22

CONTINUATION of Chapter 21.

Verses 1-9: The ceremonially unclean priest is not to officiate or partake of the sacrificial offerings as long as he is thus defiled. The "separation" of verse 2 is explained in verses 4-6.

Verses 10-13: The particular members of the priest's family and household are mentioned as permitted to eat the offerings, while the priest himself is ceremonially defiled.

Verse 14: The need of restitution for inadvertence (cf. chap. 5:15, 16).

Verses 15, 16: The "they" may mean the priests or his relatives mentioned above.

Verses 17-25: Animals for sacrifice are to be physically perfect.

Verses 26, 27: Extreme youth regarded as equivalent to a blemish.

Verse 28: Another suggestion of humanity and kindness. (See Ex. 23: 19; Deut. 14:21; 22:6).

Verses 29, 30: One form of the Peace-offering (v. 21 and chap. 7:15).

Verses 31-33: A summary, impressing duty.

THE MESSAGE FOR MEDITATION

(1) Our best for God. "The Utmost for the Highest" (G. F. Watts). (2) "None of us liveth to himself." Others are affected by us (vv. 10-13). (3) The spirit of tender thoughtfulness in religious matters (vv. 26-28). (4) The element of freewill and spontaneity in relation to God (vv. 23, 29). (5) Redemption as the basis of sanctification (v. 33).

Leviticus 23

AFTER THE OFFERINGS, the priesthood, and the purifications, come the special occasions for worship — weekly, monthly, annually, and (chap. 25) every seventh and every fiftieth year. Stated times for approaching God are natural and inevitable. The idea of "seven" enters into all these festivals — weekly, monthly, yearly, the seventh year and fiftieth year. It is important to notice that the A.S. Version distinguishes between two Hebrew words, both of which the K. J. Version inadequately renders "feast." One is translated "set feast" (or "appointed season") by the A. S. Version, and the other "feast" (or festival). It is noteworthy that the latter word "feast" is applied to three occasions only, the feasts of Unleavened Bread, Pentecost, and Tabernacles, and it would seem that thereby these are marked out as times of special importance. It should also be noticed that five of the feasts are closely associated with harvest, thus indicating the natural aspect, while the historical element is equally emphasized.

Verses 1-3 The Weekly Sabbath. (See Gen. 2:2, 3; Exod. 16:22; 20:10; 31:13; Deut. 5:15). Two main thoughts: rest and redemption.

Verses 4, 5: The Passover. (See Exod. 12:2; Deut. 16:1-8).

Verses 6-8: The Feast of Unleavened Bread. From the beginning, this was connected with the Passover as practically one festival, but it was (as here) clearly separate in idea. The Passover was only one day; this extended to a week.

Verses 9-14: First-fruits. The commandment was given with reference to Canaan when they should arrive there.

Verses 15-22: Pentecost. One day only.

Verses 23-25: Trumpets. One day only.

Verses 26-32: Day of Atonement. See chap. 16 for details. The only *fast*. Mentioned here in connection with "the annual septenary series of sacred seasons, the final festival of which it preceded and introduced" (*Kellogg*).

Verses 33-36: Tabernacles. Appropriate after the removal of the nation's sin on the Day of Atonement.

Verses 37, 38: Summary.

Verses 39-44: Special regulations as to the Feast of Tabernacles.

THE MESSAGE FOR MEDITATION

(1) The festivals as typical of Christ. (a) The Passover and Unleavened Bread — Redemption (1 Cor. 5:7, 8), (b) Pentecost — Ingathering (Acts 2:1). (c) Trumpets — Proclamation to Israel before Christ's Coming. (d) Tabernacles — The Coming of Christ and its joy. (2) The festivals as symbolical for us. (a) Remembrance of redemption. (b) Joy in God (Psa. 89:15, harvest). (c) Worship of God. (d) Consecration ("first-fruits," James 1:18).

Leviticus 24

IT IS DIFFICULT to see the connection between this and the last chapter, especially as the next resumes and completes the teaching of chapter 23. It has been suggested that chapter 24 is parenthetical and connected with chapter 23 by the lists of the days which were associated with services at the Tabernacle. Then, too, the Feast of Tabernacles might have suggested the fruit and grain here mentioned in the oil and shewbread. The second part (concerning the blasphemer) is doubtless put here because the circumstances occurred at this time.

Verses 1-4: The Oil. Repeated from Exodus 27:20.

Verses 5-9: The Shewbread.

Verses 10-23: The incident almost certainly took place at this point. (See Ex. 21:12, 23-36). It was a lesson on the holiness of God, and a reminder of the meaning of the oft-repeated statement, "I am the Lord."

THE MESSAGE FOR MEDITATION

(1) The two types: (a) the oil, the Holy Spirit (Psa. 43:3; Rev. 1:12-20; 2:1); (b) the shewbread, Christ as the Bread of God for the life of man (John 6:32-51). (2) The two symbols: (a) Our need of light, first in and then through us. (See Zech. 4:4 to 14; Matt. 5:14, 16). (b) Our readiness to be a blessing to others, the bread of their lives. (3) The solemn lesson — "holy and reverend is His Name" (Psa. 111:9). God's Fatherhood is to produce awe (1 Pet. 1:17).

Leviticus 25

RESUMPTION of Subject of Chapter 23 and Completion of the System of Festivals. The sacred "seven" is again evident.

Verses 1-7: The Sabbatic year (Deut. 15:1-11; 31:10-13).

Verses 8-55: The Jubilee Year. The Hebrew word for trumpet is *yobel,* and perhaps the name was due to the way in which the year was announced. The Latin *jubilate* carries the idea of rejoicing.

This section is divided thus: verses 8 to 12, the ordinance itself; verses 13-28, the law of the jubilee year in relation to property in land; verses 29-34, in relation to property in houses; verses 35-55, in relation to property in slaves. (See Exod. 21:2).

The Message for Meditation

(1) God's claim. The sabbatical and jubilee years were a constant reminder of God's right to the people and their possessions and time (cf. v. 23, "Mine" — "Ye are not your own"). (2) God's bounty. These institutions declared God's wonderful provision for the people. The keyword of the year of jubilee is "liberty." (3) God's example. We, too, should be bountiful, "ready to distribute." "God loves a *hilarious* giver" (2 Cor. 9:7, *Greek*). (4) God's foreshadowing. These years spoke of Christ the "Goel," or Kinsman-Redeemer (v. 49; Ruth 2:1; 3:10-18; 4:1-19), and tell of His final and complete redemption, and its permanent blessing of liberty. (See Isa. 61: 1, 2; Luke 4:18, 19).

Leviticus 26

A chapter of Spiritual Applications. In reality, the last chapter of Leviticus; chapter 27 being an appendix.

Verses 1, 2: Introductory of summary of duty, which is indicated as threefold.

Verses 3-13: The Blessings of Obedience: plenty (vv. 4, 5), peace (v. 6), protection (v. 6), power (vv. 7, 8), prosperity (v. 9), provision (v. 10), privilege (vv. 11-13).

Verses 14-39: The Results of Disobedience. The sections are: 14-17; 18-20; 21, 22; 23-26; 27-39. The "seven times" of verses 18, 21, 24, 27, refers to *degree* of punishment, not to *duration.* The divine judgments would be intensified. Mark the fulfilment of all this in Israel's history, especially the survival of the people while scattered, and the uncultivated and sparsely populated condition of the country.

Verses 40-46: Repentance and Restoration. Only partially fulfilled on the return from Babylon; waiting complete realization in the future.

THE MESSAGE FOR MEDITATION

(1) The alternatives for us. Blessing on obedience; judgment on disobedience. Mark the contrast in Psalm 1 between the man "as a tree," steadfast, fresh, and fruitful — and the man "as chaff," rootless, lifeless, and useless. (2) The past, present, and future of Israel. Scripture is full of it. (See Zech. 12:8-14; 13:1; Rev. 1:7; Rom. 11:2, 15).

Leviticus 27

AN APPLICATION dealing with vows. Hitherto, matters treated have been obligatory; now they are voluntary (Deut. 23:22). These instructions are to regulate the spontaneous action of the worshipper.

Verses 2-8: Vows as to Persons.

Verses 9-13: As to Animals.

Verses 14, 15: As to Houses.

Verses 16-24: As to Lands.

Verse 25: The Standards of Calculation.

Verses 26-33: The Matters Excluded from Vows. These are because they are already the Lord's.

Verse 34: The Closing Summary of the Book.

THE MESSAGE FOR MEDITATION

(1) Vows in the Old Testament. We think of religion in those days as wholly and purely obligatory, but there are many instances of voluntary vows (e.g., Gen. 28:20-22; Num. 30:2; Deut. 33:21). The only requirement was faithfulness to vows (Eccles. 5:5). (2) Today, while vows are no necessary part of Christianity, God loves and rejoices in every expression of our voluntary devotion. The New Testament has ample room and a large welcome for spontaneity in religion, as proving the existence and power of love (Rom. 12:1). Love in the New Testament is not a feeling, but a fact; not a sentiment, but a sacrifice; not an emotion, but an energy. "God so loved that He gave."

6

THE BOOK OF NUMBERS

INTRODUCTION

I. THE TITLE

Our word "Numbers" or "Numberings" comes from the Greek *Arithmoi* (Numbers, plural), and refers to the two "numberings" of the people, in the second year after leaving Egypt (chap. 1) and in the fortieth year (chap. 26). The Hebrew title, "In the Wilderness" describes the contents, while the first word "and" connects it with the preceding books as the continuation of them.

II. THE PURPOSE

When Israel's position as the people of God had been regulated by the laws found in Exodus and Leviticus, they were to advance into Canaan, which was only fifteen days' march from Sinai. But the circumstances recorded in this book hindered this consummation of the divine purpose, and the result was a delay of nearly forty years.

Numbers gives the account of their wilderness experiences, especially of those that need not and should not have happened.

III. THE CHARACTER

Except for the fifteen months at Sinai, this book tells all that is known for forty years (1:1; 33:38; 36:13). The silence of the thirty-eight years is thus in marked contrast with the fulness of the record at Sinai. The Tabernacle was the rallying-point, and the names in chapter 33 are probably those of its stations during the years of wandering. The blending of history and legislation is true to life, and, as in Exodus and Leviticus, the laws grew out of the experiences of the people. But since Leviticus does not advance the history (apart from the two brief historical incidents recorded), this links the book of Numbers to the narrative of Exodus.

IV. THE CONTENTS

There are two general divisions, marked by the two organizations (chaps. 1 and 26). The first muster was of the generation which came out of Egypt (chaps. 1 to 25), but it ended in disaster. Then came the second (chaps. 26 to 36), consisting of the new generation. But closer study reveals details which indicate the substance more clearly, and the following outline represents the results of comparing and blending several authorities.

1. *Organization.* Preparation for Advance — at Sinai (chaps. 1 to 10).
   a. The arrangement of the camp (chaps. 1 to 4).
   b. The purity of the camp (chaps. 5 and 6).
   c. The worship of the camp (chaps. 7:1 to 9:14).
   d. The progress of the camp (chaps. 9:15 to 10:36).
2. *Disorganization.* Check to Advance — Sinai to Kadesh (chaps. 11 to 25).
   a. Discontent and distrust (chaps. 11 and 12).
   b. Disobedience and disaster (chaps. 13 and 14).
   c. Discipline and death (chaps. 15 to 25).
3. *Reorganization.* Renewal of Advance — Kadesh again (chaps. 26 to 36).
   a. New census (chap. 26).
   b. New experiences (chaps. 27, 31, 32).
   c. New laws (chaps. 28-30, 33-36).

V. THE TYPICAL TEACHING

Some writers speak of this Book as indicative of the Christian *walk* as distinct from his *worship* (Leviticus). But this does not seem to be spiritually correct, for it is a record of *wandering* through disobedience, and as Israel was not intended to pass thirty-eight years in the wilderness, so the Christian is not expected to have wilderness experiences through disobedience, but to pass straight from Redemption (Egypt), Instruction (Exodus) and Worship (Leviticus), to the full Christian life (Canaan, Joshua).

There are some types of Christ which call for special attention. See 1 Corinthians 10:1-11.
1. The Nazarite (chap. 6).
2. The Red Heifer (chap. 19).
3. The Bread (11:7-9, as in Exod. 16).

4. The Water (20:11, as in Exod. 17).
5. The Brazen Serpent (chap. 21).
6. The Star (24:17, cf. Rev. 22:16).
7. The Cities of Refuge.

VI. THE MESSAGE

The main thoughts are (1) Human Failure, and (2) Divine Faithfulness. As Leviticus and Hebrews should be studied together for *doctrine,* so Numbers and Hebrews should be studied together for *duty.*[1] The following are the main points:

1. *God's Purpose.* The people were intended to go at once to Canaan. This symbolizes (not Heaven) but the Christian life in its fulness of blessing (Ephesians).

2. *God's Requirement.* Just trust and obedience — these were all.

3. *God's Provision.* Sacrifice, Priests, Pillar of Cloud and Fire, a Leader, food and protection ample for all needs.

4. *God's Disappointment.* Because of fear versus faith, and this was due to self versus God (13:26-33).

5. *God's Chastisement.* Kept out of blessing thirty-eight years. God is not partial, but strict with His children.

6. *God's Forbearance.* He did not leave them, because He remembered His covenant.

7. *God's Call Today.* Hebrews gives the message in its five interposed warnings. (1) 2:1-4, against drifting; (2) 3:6 to 4:13, against disbelieving; (3) 5:11 to 6:21, against degenerating; (4) 10:36-39, against despising; (5) 12:25-29, against departing. The keyword of Numbers is Unbelief, and this is seen in its spiritual counterpart in Hebrews. See especially Hebrews 3:7 to 4:12. In Numbers the people drew back; in Hebrews we see the spiritual result (10:38). And so Hebrews 11:6 sums up Numbers.

> They came to the gates of Canaan,
>   But they never entered in!
> They came to the very threshold,
>   But they perished in their sin.
>
> On the morrow they would have entered,
>   But God had shut the gate;
> They wept, they rashly ventured,
>   But alas! it was too late.

1. See the Author's volume "Let Us Go On," *op. cit.*

And so we are ever coming
To the place where two ways part;
One leads to the land of promise,
And one to a hardened heart.

CHAPTER STUDIES

Numbers 1

Verse 1: Closely connected with Exodus, chapter 40, as the continuance of the history.

Verses 2-16: The Census Commanded by God. The figures were taken from the family registrations. Every citizen would be regarded as a soldier unless proved to be disqualified (v. 3). The tribes are mentioned apparently in the order of their encampment afterward, south, east, west and north. Gad's position seems to be recorded, so as to associate him with the other sons of the handmaids, and after those of Leah and Rachel. "Thousands" (v. 16) is used for families in Judges 6:15.

Verses 17-46: The Census Taken. This was done by God's order (v. 19) and thus was different from that of David. There was nothing wrong in a census in itself. In comparing verse 46 with Exodus 38:26, there seems to have been an increase of 13,000 since the departure from Egypt.

Verses 47-54: The Levites were numbered separately (3:39).

THE MESSAGE FOR MEDITATION

(1) God has an enrollment of His children (Luke 10:20; Rev. 3:5; 21:27). (2) God has need of fit men in His service (v. 3). (3) God knows exactly who are His (2 Tim. 2:19). (4) God has a place for each one — "To every man *his* work."

Numbers 2

THE ARRANGEMENT of the Camp.

Verses 1, 2: The command was that the people should pitch according to tribes and families.

Verses 3-9: The East Side: Three Tribes. The post of honor as leader was given to the tribe of Judah, probably because of the anticipation of the Messiah coming from thence (Gen. 49:10).

Verses 10-16: The South Side: Three Tribes.

Verse 17: The Tabernacle in the Center.

Verses 18-24: The West Side: Three Tribes. Behind the Tabernacle.

Verses 25-31: The North Side: Three Tribes.

Verses 32-34: Summary. The four-square arrangement suggests Ezekiel 48:20 and Revelation 21:16.

THE MESSAGE FOR MEDITATION

(1) God is a God of order (1 Cor. 14:33, 40; 15:23). (2) Unity in diversity is a great principle of life (Eph. 4:7-12). (3) The presence of God (in the center) is the rallying-point for the whole Church (Psa. 46:5). (4) Spiritual symmetry is to be cultivated, never anything one-sided or unequal (Rev. 21:16).

Numbers 3

THE ARRANGEMENT of the Host, continued.

Verses 1-4: The Priests. "Generations" as in Genesis 2:4, looking forward, describing posterity. Another reference to the sin of Nadab and Abihu. There are five of these in Leviticus and Numbers, showing the emphasis laid on it.

Verses 5-13: The Levites. They were separated for the purpose of being substituted for the first-born (v. 12, Exod. 13:2).

Verses 14-24: The Families of the Three Sons of Levi.

Verses 25-39: The work in relation to the Tabernacle assigned to the various families of the tribe of Levi.

Verses 40-51: The redemption of the first-born as substituted by the Levites.

THE MESSAGE FOR MEDITATION

(1) The solemn emphasis on obedience as seen in the renewed reference to Nadab and Abihu. (2) The great importance of details as shown by the full instructions. (3) The variety in the work of God's people as indicated by the information about the three families. (4) The elaborate precaution suggesting holiness, as evidenced by the restriction of the Tabernacle to the Levites. (5) The definite call to consecration as marked by the reference to the first-born.

Numbers 4

The Duties of the Levites at the Tabernacle Service, in Detail.

Verses 1-15: The Kohathites and Their Part.

Verses 16-20: The Work of Eleazar. "Thus do," as in verses 5-15.

Verses 21-28: The Gershonites and Their Duties.

Verses 29-33: The Merarites and Their Place.

Versus 34-49: The fulfilment of these divine commands by Moses and Aaron.

The Message for Meditation

(1) The variety of gifts and duties in the Church of God (Eph. 4:7-12; 1 Cor. 12). There is work for all (encouragement) and for each (humility). (2) The character of the God we serve ("lest they die," v. 20; see Heb. 12; 28, 29).

Numbers 5

The two next chapters deal with the Purity of the Camp.

Verses 1-4: The Removal of the Unclean (Lev. 13 to 15; 19 and 21).

Verses 5-10: The Restitutions after Trespasses (Lev. 6:1-7).

Verses 11-31: The Requirements in Cases of Jealousy and Adultery. See Leviticus 20:10. These elaborate details were perhaps intended as a protection against unjust and sudden divorce. A striking illustration of God's wisdom and justice.

The Message for Meditation

(1) The constant and varied reminders of the need of holiness. (2) The close relation of holiness to the presence and character of God; "in the midst whereof I dwell" (v. 4). (3) The conditions of acceptance are always sacrifice and purification (vv. 5-10). (4) The great principle of restitution, to man and to God.

Numbers 6

Verses 1-21: The Law of the Nazirite (not Nazarite, cf. A.S.V.). The person (of either sex) was entirely separated to the Lord. The abstinence from wine and the long hair were outward symbols of this consecration. Does the former mean the surrender of natural joy? (Psa. 104:15). But the abstinence extended to things pleasant and not merely intoxicating (v. 4). And did the latter mean the readiness to be counted a reproach for the Lord's sake? (1 Cor. 11:14). Or was it merely a sign of virility? (Judges 16:17). Verses 13-21 indicate what was to be done when the period of the vow was over and the vow was discharged.

Verses 22-27: The Priestly Benediction. The threefold use of "Lord" with the singular "name" (v. 27) suggests, perhaps faintly foreshadows, the Trinity in Unity. The "name" of God is always the "nature" or revealed character, that which is known of Him. The priests were only the visible exponents of the divine reality which came direct from God ("They . . . I" v. 27). See an elaboration in Psalm 121.

THE MESSAGE FOR MEDITATION

(1) Consecration means that every power, every privilege, and every possibility belongs to God. (2) Benediction means (a) actual benefaction and constant *preservation* (v. 24); (b) the favor of God as shown in His *grace* (v. 25); and (c) the fellowship of God which is experienced in *peace* (v. 26). "The blessing of the Lord it maketh rich" (see Luke 24:50, 51; Acts 3:26. For the New Testament counterpart, see 2 Cor. 13:14).

Numbers 7

THE GIFTS of the Princes.

Verses 1-3: The Offer. The princes were doubtless heads of the tribes, as in chapter 1:4.

Verses 1-88: One of the longest chapters in the Bible — and the gifts are all identical.

Verse 89: The Summary, indicating the special privilege of Moses in his approach to God.

THE MESSAGE FOR MEDITATION

(1) God loves spontaneous giving. (2) God recognizes every gift. "Though the offerings of the princes were identical, each is separately recorded (Mark 12: 41-44)" (Scofield). The

minute detail shows that no gift is forgotten or overlooked. (3) God welcomes thoughtful and useful gifts; these were mainly to facilitate the transportation of the Tabernacle. (4) God crowns life with fellowship involving revelation and intercourse (v. 89).

Numbers 8

FURTHER INSTRUCTIONS as to Proper Worship.

Verses 1-4: The light in the Tabernacle (Exod. 25:37; 27:21; 37:17; 40:25).

Verses 5-26: The cleansing of the Levites for their work (see chapter 3); v. 19 is very striking. The Levites were to "make atonement" for the people. How could they do it? Not by sacrifice, which the priests alone could offer, but by their *service*. They were representatives of the people, and as such, their service was, as it were, substitutionary. This was the one exception to the requirement of blood-shedding in sacrifice (see 25:11, 13 and Psa. 106:30, 31). "The priests made an atonement by sacrifice; the Levites by attendance" (*Matthew Henry*).

THE MESSAGE FOR MEDITATION

(1) Light-bearing (vv. 1-4) is a very special form of service (Matt. 5:14-16). (2) Service means consecration. (3) Service is based on sacrifice. (4) Service calls for cleansing. (5) "They also serve who only stand and wait" (cf. v. 24).

Numbers 9

Verses 1-5: The Passover. This was just before they left Sinai (Exod. 12; Lev. 23).

Verses 6-14: (cf. Lev. 21:1). An instance of the "sweet reasonableness" of God's law, of the power of the spirit over the letter.

Verses 15-23: The cloud (Exod. 40:34). The sign of God's guidance.

THE MESSAGE FOR MEDITATION

(1) The Passover was a memory of the past, a realization of the present, and an anticipation of the future. So is the Lord's Supper; it contains the whole gospel. (2) The problems of difficulty are to be taken to God in prayer (v. 8). (3) The

guidance of God is to be followed step by step, whether in journeying or in waiting. The great principle is according to "the commandment of the Lord" (vv. 18, 19, 20, 23). (4) God's will involves two things: *where* and *when,* and He will make both clear to the obedient.

Numbers 10

Verses 1-10: The silver trumpets. Not the same as the jubilee trumpets (Lev. 25:9); different terms are used. They were intended for several purposes (vv. 2-7, 9, 10).

Verses 11-28: The first journey from Sinai, with a halt in Paran.

Verses 29-32: The relation of Hobab to Moses is uncertain, because "father-in-law" is a general term for relation by marriage. Raguel is Reuel in Exodus 2:18. Moses made two pleas: (1) an invitation (v. 29), and when this was refused (2) an appeal (v. 31), which was accepted (Judges 4:11).

Verses 33-36: The departure detailed, already summarized in v. 12. The morning and evening prayers of Moses.

THE MESSAGE FOR MEDITATION

1) The trumpets were twofold: (a) A summons to man (vv. 2-7); (b) An appeal to God (vv. 9-10). May not these suggest the *Word* and *prayer?* (2) The message of Moses (v. 29) is appropriate to the Christian today in relation to others: Testimony ("we"); Invitation ("come"); Promise ("we will"); Reason ("for"). This fourfold appeal should always be made by us, and it will be, if we have such clear assurance of and complete confidence in God as Moses had. (3) The two prayers of Moses were — for (a) the divine protection by day; and (b) the divine presence by night.

Numbers 11

EXPERIENCES on the Journey.

Verses 1-3: This was very soon after leaving Sinai. The murmuring was visited with punishment, unlike Exodus 15:22 and 16:2, because the people had become more deeply responsible through fuller revelation of God's power.

Verses 4-9: Further trouble came, through the people who followed Israel out of Egypt (perhaps half-breeds, Lev. 24: 10). Their influence was soon communicated to Israel. The remembrance of the luxuries (v. 5) was probably an exaggeration. It also differs from the cause of the former murmurings — starvation (Exod. 16:2).

Verses 10-15: Moses was affected by this outburst, and he fell into sin. He exaggerated his responsibility (v. 12) and forgot himself.

Verses 16-25: God's forbearance met this petulant outburst by providing help for Moses. These elders are not the same as those in Exodus 18:21. The former were for secular work; the latter for religious. God also gave a message for the people (vv. 18-20) to which Moses replied with a fresh expression of temper, and allowed himself to utter words (v. 22) that were wholly improper, especially after such an event as Exodus 16:13. But God again met His erring servant with lovingkindness and forbearance (v. 23).

Verses 26-30: The irregular prophecy by Eldad and Medad was a surprise to Joshua, but the reply of Moses shows that his relations with God had become re-established; and, in his characteristic freedom from self-seeking and ambition, he deprecates the sincere but mistaken zeal of his young servant.

Verses 31-35: God then dealt with the people. The "two cubits" of v. 31 were the height or level of the flight of the birds, so that they could be easily captured. There is no reference (as sceptics often urge) to the idea of the quails being piled two cubits deep. The "spreading abroad" (v. 32) was for drying ready for food. But the punishment for the unwarranted murmuring quickly followed, and the place was significantly and sadly called "The Graves of Greediness," or "strong desire."

THE MESSAGE FOR MEDITATION

(1) Sin springs from short memories. The people complained soon after seeing God's wonderful power and glory. (2) Discontent springs from distrust and is a terrible peril. (3) Influence of outsiders may affect the spirituality of Christian people (v. 4). (4) Spiritual life may be lowered by strain and stress, yet it is wrong that it should become thus lowered (v. 11). (5) God is very pitiful and of tender mercy to His

erring children (see 1 Kings 19:5-7). (6) The gifts of the Spirit cannot be limited or monopolized (v. 28). (7) Large-heartedness rejoices in evidence of the Spirit in others (v. 29).

Numbers 12

THE MURMURING of Miriam and Aaron against Moses.

Verses 1, 2: Two grounds of complaint: (1) Moses' marriage (v. 1); (2) Moses' monopoly of divine revelations. The marriage was obviously not that to Zipporah the Midianite, which was not likely to be a contention so long after. It was a new marriage, to one, probably, of the "mixed multitude" (11:4), and there was nothing absolutely wrong in it, the matter being purely personal to Moses. But Miriam probably felt that her influence with her brother had gone, or become lessened. She was evidently the leading spirit. The cause was characteristically feminine, and she was the only one punished. Aaron had been led by her. He was always weak and easily influenced. The second ground of complaint was colored by the fact that Aaron would be the recipient of revelations through being a priest, and she by being a prophetess (Exod. 15).

Verse 3: An explanation of the true character of Moses, doubt-less inserted later by an editor, to show the groundlessness of the charge, as shown in the absence of pride.

Verses 4-8: God's vindication of Moses, who is shown (v. 7) to be wholly different from (and superior to) the prophet, and therefore to Miriam (see Exod. 33:11).

Verses 9-15: The punishment of Miriam, the plea of Aaron, and the intercession of Moses. But the wrong could not be wholly overlooked. Even an earthly father's action would imply shame (v. 14); much more was it necessary to show God's displeasure.

THE MESSAGE FOR MEDITATION

(1) Jealousy among Christian workers is sad and perilous. (2) Silence is the best way of meeting false charges. (3) God will champion His own and His people's honor. (4) God only asks for faithfulness in service (Heb. 3:1-6): "Be thou faithful" — "good and faithful servant."

Numbers 13

THE REBELLION at Kadesh is recorded in this and the next chapter, which thus form a complete whole.

Verses 1-16: The spies sent. The idea came originally from the people, and God granted the request (Deut. 1:20-25). The names of the spies (apart from Caleb and Joshua) are not found elsewhere. The tribe of Levi had no representative, because of its unique position as not possessing any territory.

Verses 17-20: The instructions of Moses were to reassure the people; for, of course, he and others knew well what the land was.

Verses 21-25: The journey extended from the extreme south to the farthest north.

Verses 26-33: The report. All agreed as to the fruitfulness, and proved it by what they brought back (vv. 26, 27), but the statement about the inhabitants and cities (v. 28) was exaggerated. In v. 32, "catcth up" seems to mean that wars were frequent between the various peoples and by incursions from neighboring nations, so that there was a constant loss of life.

THE MESSAGE FOR MEDITATION

(1) Failure to trust God and His word led to the request for the spies (Deut. 1). God had promised Canaan without question or qualification. (2) The difference of standpoint between the Ten and the Two. The former saw the giants and forgot God. The latter saw God and feared not the giants. (3) The splendid courage of faith in the face of difficulties and dangers. "Let us go up at once . . . for we are well able" (v. 30). (4) The habit of looking at the dark side always means weakness, and leads to doubt, depression, despondency, disbelief, and despair.

Numbers 14

Verses 1-4: The reception of the report by the people. This was the extremity of all their rebellions (v. 4). Hitherto they had wished to go back or to have died in Egypt; but never before had they actually proposed to return.

Verses 5-9: Moses and Aaron were horrified at this behavior, and Joshua and Caleb were also greatly concerned and pleaded with the people to trust and obey God and not to fear. In v. 9 "bread" means "easily captured."

Verses 10-12: But the people were callous and cruel, and God interposed, offering to set them aside and make Moses the head of a nation.

Verses 13-16: The reply of Moses is significant. He has no ambition for himself, but speaks of what others will think of God if they do not reach Canaan.

Verses 17-19: Then came a prayer for pardon based on God's character. Mark the twofold greatness — power (v. 17) and mercy (v. 19).

Verses 20-25: The pardon is at once granted, but the action cannot be overlooked; they are to remain in the wilderness.

Verses 26-38: After God's answer to Moses' prayer, comes this second and general announcement, spoken to Aaron as well, and intended to be passed on to the people (v. 30); "doubtless" is *without doubt.*

Verses 39-45: The divine decision led to grief, and the people went to the opposite extreme. From unbelief they went to presumption, and so from mourning and murmuring they swung over to rashness. But the action was both futile and fatal. God was not with them (vv. 42, 44), and their enemies attacked and defeated them.

THE MESSAGE FOR MEDITATION

(1) Doubt which led to depression, despondency, disbelief, and despair is now seen to go on to disobedience and disaster. (2) God's best could have been enjoyed in fifteen days; but He was compelled to delay it for thirty-eight years. (3) The nobility of Moses' character, in disregarding his own glory, and thinking only of God's reputation in the eyes of the world. (4) God's pardon does not always remove the consequences of wrongdoing. (5) The inspired commentary on these chapters is Hebrews 3:7 to 4:13, with its twofold message: (a) "Harden not your hearts" (3:7 to 4:2); (b) "Hear His voice" (4:3-13).

Numbers 15

THE THIRTY-EIGHT years in the wilderness begin here. It is important to remember that while the journey from Egypt to Sinai was part of God's plan for Israel, the years of wandering were wholly outside His will, because they were due to disobedience. The chapters from 15 to 25 give all the knowledge we possess of this long period. God cast a veil of silence over these years, while the old generation was dying out and the new one was being trained. The only historical incident recorded is in chapter 16, and even this is without any note of time or place. Bare hints (all we possess) of this period are given in Deuteronomy 8:2-6; 29:5, 6; Joshua 5:4-8; Ezekiel 20:10-26; Amos 5:25, 26; Acts 7:42, 43. The names in chapter 33 may refer to the places where the Tabernacle rested during these years of wandering. It has been suggested that chapter 15 anticipates the end of this barren period and gives instructions for the life in Canaan. But no date is given.

Verses 1-31: The Offerings. Unwitting sins are provided for by atonement, but there was no atonement for presumptuous wrong-doing (v. 30).

Verses 32-36: Judgment on Disobedience.

Verses 37-41: A Reminder of the Need of Obedience. The word "fringes" is thought by some to mean "tassels."

THE MESSAGE FOR MEDITATION

(1) The sad results of a believer's disobedience (see note 1 in Scofield Bible). (2) The strong emphasis on careful adherence to instructions. (3) Verses 32-36 illustrate Hebrews 10:31"It is a fearful thing to fall into the hands of the living God." (4) Verses 37-41 exemplify the three principles of remembrance, testimony and obedience. The believer is a "marked man" (Gal. 6:17).

Numbers 16

"THE GAINSAYING of Korah" (Jude 11).

Verses 1-3: The Bold Assertion (see Heb. 5:4). The most serious of all the revolts against Moses and Aaron.

Verses 4-7: The Confident Challenge. Korah was evidently the leader.

Verses 8-11: The Solemn Rebuke. The opposition was really against God, not against Moses.

Verses 12-15: The Rejected Appeal. This was the second part of the revolt, and associated with Korah. The two lines were thus combined, one against Moses as leader and the other against

Aaron as Priest. The reference to "eyes" (v. 14) is probably symbolical of deception — "wilt thou throw dust in their eyes?"

Verses 16-22: The Divine Vindication. In the confirmation of the priesthood lay the very existence of God's purpose and organization for the people.

Verses 23-35: The Awful Punishment. The children of Korah were for some reason exempted (26:9-11; Psa. 88; 1 Chron. 6).

Verses 36-40: The Definite Lesson. A constant reminder was instituted.

Verses 41-50: The Murmuring People. Evidently they were in sympathy with Korah.

THE MESSAGE FOR MEDITATION

Five pictures: (1) Korah. The sin of presumption (Psa. 19:13) for which there was no sacrifice (see 15:30), and which, like many other sins, seriously affects others. (2) Moses. The consciousness of innocence, humbly and confidently leaving everything to God. (3) God. The interposition on behalf of His servants, His own word and His glory (Psa. 105:14, 15). (4) The People. Secret sympathy and then open agreement with Korah in spite of everything that had happened. (5) Aaron. The priestly mediation. Standing between the living and the dead — Christ's position and (as far as is possible) ours in Him.

Numbers 17

GOD'S VINDICATION of Aaron and the Priesthood, following the Rebellion and Rebuke.

Verses 1-5: The Divine Instructions. The test would prove.

Verses 6-9: The Divine Confirmation. The "almonds" (v. 8) blossom with great alacrity (Jer. 1:11) and perhaps were intended to be a signal proof of God's power.

Verses 10-12: The Divine Purpose. A permanent reminder.

Verses 12, 13: The People's Recognition. Awed by what had occurred.

THE MESSAGE FOR MEDITATION

(1) Christ alone is God's High Priest (John 14:6; Acts 4:12). (2) Christ alone is living. The spiritual vitality and fruitfulness based on resurrection from the dead. (3) Christ as sole and living High Priest, testifying to and recognized by man (Heb. 4:14 to 5:10).

Numbers 18

REGULATIONS for the Priesthood. Clearly connected with the rebellion of Korah (v. 5).

Verses 1-7: The Responsibility of the Priests. Addressed to Aaron only, not, as is usual, to Moses, or to Moses and Aaron (2:1; 4:1; 19:1). To "bear the iniquity of the sanctuary" (v. 1) means to be responsible for all sins connected with the Tabernacle, such as those of Nadab, Abihu, and Korah.

Verses 8-24: The Maintenance of the Priesthood. The Levites had no territory as the other tribes had (v. 20).

Verses 25-32: Addressed to Moses only, probably because it was a matter between priests and Levites which would be more suitable for him to announce. In v. 28 "the Levites tithed the people and the priests tithed the Levites."

THE MESSAGE FOR MEDITATION

(1) The possibility of sin even in the holiest service. (2) The wonderful privilege of being representatives of men to God. (3) The responsibilities of office. (4) The duty of maintaining the ministry (1 Cor. 9:13, 14). (5) The glorious position of all God's people today (see verse 20, "I am thy part and thy inheritance" (Psa. 16:5; Ezek. 44:28; Titus 2:14, where "peculiar" means "specially His own"). "As the priests were the special possession of the Lord, so the Lord was the special possession of the priests." This means Safety, Sufficiency, and Satisfaction.

Numbers 19

THE ORDINANCE of the Red Heifer.

Verses 1-10: The fulness of the symbolism is very striking. Redness suggests the color of blood. Freedom from blemish indicates the perfection needed for sacrifice. Then came (1) the slaying; (2) the sprinkling of the blood; (3) the burning; (4) the preservation of the ashes for use in ceremonial purification. All through, a great emphasis is laid on death and its connection with sin. The reference to the priest (vv. 3, 4) is due to the need for the High Priest to avoid the performance of ceremonies which caused uncleanness. Outside the camp (v. 3) meant a special stress on separation and uncleanness (see Heb. 13:12).

Verses 11-22: One form of uncleanness was by contact with death — indicating its repugnance to God. The "water of purification" (vv. 13, 20, 21) means the water that symbolically removed pollution.

THE MESSAGE FOR MEDITATION

(1) The solemn emphasis on death (Rom. 6:21). Death always means separation. Death as separation is threefold: (a) physical death, the separation of the soul from the body; (b) spiritual death, the separation of the soul from God; (c) everlasting death, the separation of the soul and body from God forever. (2) The great principles of true life are defilement by contact and purification by separation (2 Cor. 6:17). (3) The special spiritual meaning of the Antitype, Christ. The sacrifice shows that water was not enough for cleansing, and the red heifer as a type of Christ means cleansing from defilement (Heb. 9:14). By dying He purifies from all that death implies and involves of uncleanness.

Numbers 20

FROM KADESH to HOR.

Verse 1: Death of Miriam. The brevity is perhaps significant. Her life is a curious blend of faithfulness and unfaithfulness.

Verses 2-5: A Fresh Murmuring (see Exodus 17). The people were constantly being tested.

Verse 6: The Action of Moses and Aaron (see 14:5).

Verses 7, 8: God's Command. No rebuke is given. Forbearance is again manifested.

Verses 9-11: The Error of Moses was threefold: (1) The temper indicated by calling the people "rebels" which, though true, was not warranted; (2) the suggestion that he and Aaron were the givers of the water ("we"); (3) the striking of (instead of speaking to) the rock. (N.B. The type was thus spoiled. Christ was "struck" only once. See also Psalm 106:32, 33.)

Verses 12, 13: The Divine Punishment. God's character before the people had been involved.

Verses 14-21: The Request to Edom, and its refusal (Gen. 36:31). Kinship had no influence.

Verses 22-29: The Death of Aaron. The absence of details is perhaps a hint of Aaron's failure toward the close of his life.

THE MESSAGE FOR MEDITATION

(1) The peril of disbelief. The new generation was as sinful as the old, and even after all God had done they could not trust Him. (2) The peril of disobedience. Even God's children may do wrong. Moses fell at his strong point of meekness. The saddest part was the wrong impression he gave of God. So may believers do today. (3) The peril of discouragement. Edom's refusal was doubtless a severe blow. David shows the right spirit in such circumstances — he encouraged himself in God (1 Sam. 30:6). (4) The peril of distrust. Aaron's life was marked by great weakness which led to failure, and all because he did not put (and keep) God first.

Numbers 21

EPISODES on the Way.

Verses 1-3: Victory over Arad. Arad is the name of a man (1 Chron. 8:15) and of a place (Josh. 12:14). The territory was part of the southern-most area of the Canaanites. (On vows, see Lev. 27:28; cf. Gen. 28:20).

Verses 4-9: The Brazen Serpent. Discouragement after victory led to murmuring, and this in turn brought on severe punishment. The intercession of Moses was sought and gained, and the healing came through the likeness of the cause of the trouble (see Rom. 8:3). N. B. Cf. homeopathy whose principle is "like cures like").

Verses 10-20: The Journeying. The book (v. 14) is unknown. The song of joy (v. 17) seems to have been included in it.

Verses 21-32: Victory over the Amorites. The history is continued from v. 13, vv. 14-20 being a digression. For Amorites, see Genesis 10:16; 15:16. Chemosh (v. 29) was the god of the Moabites.

Verses 33-35: Victory over Og.

THE MESSAGE FOR MEDITATION

(1) Victory, three times: 1-3; 21-32; 33-35. Its possibility (a) even after frequent failure; (b) because of faithfulness to God; (c) shown in courage and faith (v. 34). (2) Discouragement is often due to the severity and length of the journey of life. But it is a constant cause of sin. (3) The typical character of the story of the serpents: (a) Sin; (b) Suffering; (c) Sorrow; (d) Suppli-

cation; (e) Salvation (John 3:14, 15; 2 Cor. 5:21). The look of faith was at once simple, searching (as a test), saving, and satisfying.

Numbers 22

Chapters 22 to 24 record the story of Balaam.

Verses 1-6: Moab's Fear of Israel and the First Embassy to Balaam. Evidently he was a survivor of the true religion outside the line of Abraham. The "river" (v. 5) is the Euphrates, showing the long distance they went.

Verses 7-12: The Appeal to God and its Answer.

Verses 13-20: The Second Embassy. Balak's special appeal and Balaam's attitude.

Verses 21-35: The Divine Permission and its Sequel. The circumstances are capable of explanation only as miraculous.

Verses 36-44: The Meeting of Balaam and Balak.

The Message for Meditation

(1) Balak's threefold testimony: to the people of God (v. 3); to religion (v. 5), sending to Balaam instead of fighting Israel; to idolatry (v. 6), the uselessness of his own gods. (2) Balaam's threefold conflict: (a) Knowledge and will — he knew about Israel and yet he wanted to go. (b) Desire and conscience. Covetousness rules though the truth was clear (v. 12). Mark the way in which he (incorrectly) states God's word (v. 13). (c) Obedience and self-will. Why, having had a clear prohibition, did he want to know what God would "say more"? (v. 18). No new commands are ever given until and unless new circumstances arise. (3) God's threefold rebuke; (a) permission was a concession to weakness; (b) the word of God was clear (v. 12); (c) circumstances often hinder and thereby show our error (vv. 22-26).

Numbers 23

Balaam's Prophecies.

Verses 1-12: First Prophecy. The altars (v. 1) were to propitiate God. The high place (v. 3) was because it was thought necessary to see the subject of the cursing. The "parable" (Heb. *mashal*) was a proverbial (21:27) or prophetic utterance. Aram (v. 7) is Mesopotamia (Gen. 29:1). Verse 9 describes the separateness, and verse 10 the number of Israel.

Verses 13-26: Second Prophecy. The new position (v. 13) was suggested in case the former was inadequate. The utter impossibility of changing God is shown (v. 19). In v. 21 we have God's view of Israel as His covenant people, their judicial standing, not their actual state. The "unicorn" (v. 22) probably refers to some animal now extinct. The difference in Balak's words in v. 25 and v. 11 is significant. If cursing is impossible, at least blessing should be avoided.

Verses 27-30: Preparations for the third attempt.

THE MESSAGE FOR MEDITATION

(1) The evident desire of Balaam to obtain the reward (see 23:1, 15, 29). Wishes dominated actions. (2) The impossibility of altering God's will by human effort — right is always right. (3) The necessity of obedience at all costs, even though it be against our own will. (4) The futility of pious wishes (v. 10) when the life is entirely different. (5) The glory of God's people in His sight: (a) separateness (v. 9); (b) number (v. 10); (c) righteousness (v. 21 — non-imputation of sin, Psa. 32:1, 2; Gal. 3:27; Phil. 3:9); (d) protection (v. 21); (e) power (vv. 21, 22); (f) prosperity (vv. 23, 24).

Numbers 24

Verses 1-14: Third Prophecy. Balaam himself is at length convinced (v. 1), and a higher state was his experience than is seen in 23:5 and 16. The praise of Israel is full and strong (vv. 5-9). Balak's third attitude (23:11, 25) is significant (vv. 10, 11). "Advertise" (v. 14) is "advise" or "inform."

Verses 15-24: Fourth Prophecy. It is impossible to explain this fully, apart from the Messiah. The first fulfillment may be in David (vv. 17-19), but the complete realization can only be Messianic (see Gen. 49:10). Chittim (v. 24) is Cyprus (Gen. 10:4).

Verse 25: He went homeward, but not home (31:8) (see notes in Scofield Bible).

THE MESSAGE FOR MEDITATION

(1) Reluctant recognition of truth (v. 1). (2) Fine words, base wishes, and unworthy actions. (3) The judgment of Scripture

(Deut. 23:5; Josh. 13: 22; 24: 10; Micah 6:5; 2 Peter 2:15, 16; Jude 11; Rev. 2:14). (4) The characteristics of the Messiah (vv. 17-19); illumination (star); royalty (scepter); victory (smite); possession (v. 18); authority (v. 19).

Numbers 25

Verses 1-3: What Balak failed to do through Balaam, he accomplished in another way (v. 1) (see 31:16). Sensuality soon led to idolatry (v. 2). The phrase "joined unto Baal-peor" (see also v. 5) is indicative of the terrible extent of the sin (Psa. 106:28).

Verses 4, 5: The command of God to kill and expose the bodies would serve at once as a divine requirement and a manifestation to the people of the fearfulness of the sin.

Verses 6-9: The action of Phinehas led to the cessation of the trouble. The plague was evidently a resultant accompaniment of the wrong-doing. 1 Corinthians 10:8 gives 23,000 as having died in one day, while here the full number of the entire occurrence is given. Or the difference may be due to error in transcription — the Hebrew and Greek letters being used instead of figures, and thus lending themselves easily to errors in copying (see Scofield Bible on 1 Cor. 10:8).

Verses 10-13: The divine recognition of the act of Phinehas. It is very striking that it should be called an atonement. It was a vindication of righteousness. "The deed of Phinehas is the only act, neither official nor commanded, to which the power of atoning for sin is ascribed in the Old Testament" (*Pulpit Commentary*). There was also a personal reward (v. 13, Psa. 106:31).

Verses 14-18: This was not retaliation, but because Israel as God's people were His instruments.

THE MESSAGE FOR MEDITATION

(1) Aspects of Sin. (a) Victory in one way (chaps. 22 to 24) may be followed by defeat in another (v. 1). (b) The significant association of the two sins (vv. 1, 2; 1 Cor. 6:13-20). (c) The awful possibilities of evil even in God's people. (d) "The wages of sin is death" (Rom. 6:23). (2) Aspects of Atonement. (a) Based on zeal for God's glory (Heb. 10:5-10). (b) Revealing God's righteousness (Rom. 3:21-26). (c) Demonstrating God's attitude to sin. (d) Saving by substitution.

Numbers 26

THE NEW Generation.

This second numbering (chap. 1) was due to the death of all the former generation (14:29), and was made in view of their entrance into Canaan. The first census yielded a total of 603,550; this, one of 601,730. The reasons for fluctuation in numbers in particular tribes is quite unknown. The explanation of the reference to the children of Korah in v. 11 (16:32) is also unknown (see titles of Psa. 42, 88, and others).

THE MESSAGE FOR MEDITATION

(1) The consequences of sin. One numbering should have been sufficient, especially as they were so near Canaan. The sadness of sin often lies in the fact that forgiveness does not remove consequences. (2) The fresh start. A new inspiration doubtless came as they faced the future. Whatever our past, we can always "try again," and by the grace of God succeed. (3) "The Lord knoweth them that are His" (2 Tim. 2:19). It is a comfort and a cheer to realize that not one of us is forgotten of God (Psa. 87:6; Isa. 43:1; Luke 10:20).

Numbers 27

Verses 1-11: The Law of Inheritance. Probably connected with, and suggested by, the references to allotment in 26: 53-56. Zelophehad had died because of some sin of which we have no record (v. 3), and the problem was a real one; why should an inheritance pass from a family because there were no sons? God's decision is particularly interesting in the light of the position of womanhood in Christ (Gal. 3:28), and of the rights of women as now assured by law.

Verses 12-14: The death of Moses is now definitely foretold. It had been revealed to him that he was not to enter Canaan (20:12), but now he was allowed to see it. This was in answer to his own prayer (Deut. 3:25-27).

Verses 15-23: The appointment of Joshua as Moses' successor. The requirements (v. 7) are met by qualifications (v. 18), instructions (v. 19), and testimony before the people (v. 20). The difference between Moses and Joshua is very marked (v. 21). Moses was superior, Joshua subordinate to the priesthood. The Urim (and Thummim) was a way of discovering God's will (see Exod. 28:30; Lev. 8:8).

THE MESSAGE FOR MEDITATION

(1) The settlement of difficulties. Take them to God (vv. 4, 5). (2) The beauty of character. No complaint by Moses; only concern for Israel (vv. 12-16). (3) The secret of power (v. 18) — the Spirit of God. (4) The type of Christ (v. 17) — rule; leadership; care.

Numbers 28

IN CHAPTERS 28 and 29 the order of the offerings is given. It covers in rotation the whole year, and is a "legislative description of Israel's sacred year." The daily, weekly, monthly, and yearly offerings were thus systematized and prevented from being observed irregularly.

Verses 1-8: The Daily Offerings. The offerings day by day formed the basis of all else.

Verses 9, 10: The Weekly Offering. The special requirements for the Sabbath are found here for the first time.

Verses 11-15: The Monthly Offerings.

Verses 16-31: The first two of the Annual Offerings — the feasts of the Passover (vv. 16-25), of the Weeks (Pentecost, vv. 26-31), were the festivals of the Spring — as those of the Seventh month (in chap. 29) were of the Autumn. It is interesting to notice the recurrence of the idea of *seven* — days, weeks, months. Everything was based on the Sabbath idea.

THE MESSAGE FOR MEDITATION

The characteristics of the offerings are significant for our life today. They suggest: (1) God's claim on us (v. 2, "My" three times; "Me" twice). God must be first. (2) God's complete possession of us. The "fire" (v. 2) meant entire consecration. (3) God's entire satisfaction with us. The "sweet savour" meant His pleasure (Gen. 8:21; Eph. 5:2). (4) God's requirement from us. "Season" (v. 2) suggests our constant attitude to God as something appropriate to our life at all times. Notice also the seven references to the "continual burnt-offering." Romans 12:1 indicates continual consecration. We are to "keep continual festival" (1 Cor. 5:8, *Greek*).

Numbers 29

THE PARTICULAR regulation for the seventh month, the time of autumn, when there were some special features of importance in connection with the feasts.

Verses 1-6: The first day of the seventh month (Lev. 23:24).

Verses 7-11: The tenth day, the annual Day of Atonement.

Verses 12-38: The fifteenth day, the Feast of Tabernacles. The harvest being gathered, this month was one of special festivity (Exod. 23:16).

THE MESSAGE FOR MEDITATION

The special features of the seventh month. (1) A time of joy in rest after work (vv. 1, 12). The believer has joy in the Lord as he enters into the rest of faith (Matt. 11:28-30; Heb. 4:3-10). (2) A time of special consecration (vv. 2ff.). The great emphasis on the offerings suggests our life as wholly, constantly, and gladly devoted to God. (3) A time of definite atonement for sin (vv. 5,11). Amid the festivities sin was remembered and met. Our holiest and brightest life needs to be covered by the atoning blood.

Numbers 30

THE LAW of Vows for Women.

This may be an addition to Leviticus 27 or else a natural sequel to Numbers 29:37. Four cases of women's vows are mentioned: the young daughter (vv. 1-5); the betrothed woman (vv. 6-8); the widow (v.9); and the married woman (vv. 10-15). It is particularly noteworthy that the decision is to rest with the father or the husband, not with the priest. Home religion is thus emphasized. In verse 13, "afflicting the soul" may refer to fasting or some other form of self-denial. Fasting was thus connected with the Day of Atonement (Lev. 16:29; Num. 29:7).

THE MESSAGE FOR MEDITATION

Three aspects of true religion. (1) It always means absolute truth or reality towards God (Psa. 51:6). (2) It always means strict justice towards man. No one must suffer through religious vows. (3) It always means adherence to principle in relation to self. Vows like those of total abstinence or celibacy are ever to be subject to the will of God, and never based merely on our own decision.

Numbers 31

THE JUDGMENT on Midian.

Verses 1-5: The divine command (see 25:17). It was not vindictive, for vengeance, but retributive, for righteousness. Nations as such have no future life, and national sins, if followed by national punishment, must be dealt with here and now.

Verses 6-12: The High Priest could not leave because of necessary defilement (v. 19), but his son could go (16:37).

Verses 13-20: The men ought not to have brought in these captives, but left them in their own land. The women had caused trouble already, and would doubtless do so again. Israel's purity necessitated the severe action.

Verses 21-24: The earliest instance (v. 21) of the priest (not Moses) declaring what God's law was. Verse 23 adds to chapter 19 because fire would cleanse metal when water would not.

Verses 25-34: The booty and its division.

THE MESSAGE FOR MEDITATION

(1) The retribution on Balaam (vv. 8. 16). The unspeakable horror of a man who could not get his own way (chaps. 22-24) descending to counsel that brought disaster on Israel. He did not die as he (impiously) wished (23:10). (2) The righteousness of God against sin. The awfulness is seen in this judgment. (3) The response of Israel to the divine command. Prompt, full obedience is always required. (4) The recognition of God in the division of the spoil (v. 50). (5) The reward of faithfulness in the distribution of the booty.

Numbers 32

THE TWO-AND-A-HALF Tribes of East Jordan.

Verses 1-5: The choice. The land of Gilead (Gen. 37:25) is sometimes used to describe all the territory east of Jordan. The decision was unwise because of the severance it would involve. It was also perilous in view of hostile surroundings. There was no natural protection on the east such as Jordan would have been.

Verses 6-15: The rebuke. Moses had good cause for this plain and severe speaking. The action was based on a selfish disregard of the needs of their brethren. It was essentially a repetition of similar action in the past.

Verses 16-19: The rejoinder. With no resentment but with a clear recognition of the truth of Moses' rebuke, a new proposal was made.

Verses 20-24: The reply. Moses agrees to their suggestion and grants their request with a warning (v. 23).

Verse 25-27: The response. The condition is accepted.

Verses 28-32: The rest of the people are informed of the arrangement and the two-and-a-half tribes confirm their promise.

Verses 33-42: The division of the territory. In verse 33 the first mention is made of half the tribe of Manasseh becoming associated in the proposal. It is quite unknown why this tribe should have been divided.

THE MESSAGE FOR MEDITATION

(1) The choice. Actuated by selfishness and timidity. They wanted this good land, and were not prepared to go the entire length of conquest and hardship with their brethren. (2) The effect. Half-heartedness, especially among older believers, is a great discouragement to others (v. 7). (3) The need. The supreme necessity was unity in the face of Canaan. "Union is strength." The action of these tribes, with work to be done, would weaken and delay progress. When believers are at one, God's blessing always comes (Psa. 133:1). (4) The peril. Those who live on the borderland of the Church and the world, are never safe or really happy. As Gilead had no natural barriers of protection, so the half-hearted Christian is exposed to the attacks of the world. (5) The result. They not only lost fellowship, but the subsequent history shows a definite degeneration. Reuben was no longer the leading tribe, and these tribes never made a name in after-history. The timid, fearful, worldly Christian is of no service to the cause of God. And so their sin "found them out" (v. 23). Not "will be found out" but "find you out;" that is, make its mark on life, character, and influence. There is nothing sadder than spiritual degeneration.

Numbers 33

Verses 1-49: The Itinerary of the Journeyings. Verse 2, written by Moses. A clear instance of a contemporary document. Forty-two stations mentioned, twenty-four the same as in Exodus, and eighteen mentioned here only. A very scanty account of forty years. Five places are prominent: the starting-point (Egypt); the goal (Canaan); and the three special places on the way: Sinai, where the law was given; Kadesh, where the rebellion occurred; and Hor, where Aaron died.

Verses 50-56: The divine instructions as to the possession and division of Canaan. The command to dispossess is clear and its alternative plainly indicated.

THE MESSAGE FOR MEDITATION

(1) A sad reminder of sin. "What might have been" is suggested by this record. (2) A searching reminder of discipline. Step by step, God dealt with the people, testing, training, warning, leading and teaching. The future would be as the past if they were not faithful (vv. 55, 56). (3) A splendid reminder of faithfulness. God never left them, even though they were so unfaithful (2 Tim. 2:13). This is our sure refuge, the unchanging faithfulness of God (Mal. 3:6).

Numbers 34

THE PREPARATIONS for entrance into Canaan. From 33:51 to 34:29 is a complete section giving the divine instructions as to the land of Canaan and the life of Israel there.

Verses 1-12: The borders for the nine-and-a-half tribes. The geographical boundaries are not always known with exactness.

Verses 13-15: The territory of the two-and-a-half tribes (chap. 32).

Verses 16-29: The men appointed to allot the land. In v. 17, the two men were the ecclesiastical and civil heads.

THE MESSAGE FOR MEDITATION

(1) God's gift promised and its enjoyment anticipated. (2) God's assurance of possession. (3) God's care in allotting the inheritance. (4) God's method of division by priest and leader, both of them types of Christ through whom we obtain our inheritance. Read this chapter in the light of Ephesians 1:3-14.

Numbers 35

Verses 1-8: The Inheritance of the Levites. As they were set apart for special work, and had no territorial tribal inheritance, it was necessary to provide homes for them. The "suburbs" (v. 2) were enclosed spaces for pastures of cattle outside the cities. Of the forty-eight Levitical cities, six were to be cities of refuge.

Verses 9-34: Instructions as to the cities of refuge. The basis was the old custom of blood revenge, and this was the divine way of safeguarding it against wrong.

Verses 11, 12: The purpose.

Verses 13-15: The position of the cities.

Verses 16-21: The cases of murder excluded from this special provision.

Verses 22-25: The cases intended to be covered by it.

Verses 25-29: The necessity of remaining in the city until the death of the high priest. The only place where his death is associated with a special case. The explanation is not known unless, as some think, it was somehow expiatory.

Verses 30-34: Special injunctions as to murders and unwitting slayings.

THE MESSAGE FOR MEDITATION

(1) God's provision for His children (vv. 1-8). "The Lord is mindful of His own." (2) God's protection for the needy (vv. 11, 12). (3) God's righteousness against sin (vv. 16-21). (4) Christ our refuge: divinely provided, accessible, free, perfect, perpetual, conditional (vv. 26, 27).

Numbers 36

INHERITANCE of Heiresses.

Verses 1-4: The Problem. See chapter 27. The Jubilee would confirm the transfer and permanently alienate the property.

Verses 5-12: The Solution. Marriage within the tribe would settle the question.

Verse 13: Closing summary, covering the entire book.

THE MESSAGE FOR MEDITATION

(1) Trivial matters may easily involve great principles. Go deep enough, and everything in life is a moral question. (2) The certainty of our inheritance in Christ (1 Pet. 1:4). (3) The solution of all problems, great and small, is "according to the word of the Lord" (v. 5).

7

THE BOOK OF DEUTERONOMY

INTRODUCTION

I. THE TITLE

The word literally means "Second Law" but is really the equivalent of the Greek for "copy" (as in 17:18), or what we might call a "duplicate." The title given the book in the Hebrew original is taken from the first verse, "These are the words."

There is a close connection with Numbers, especially in relation to time and place (cf. Num. 36:13 with Deut. 1:1). The book continues with what took place on the first day of the eleventh month of the fortieth year in the wilderness (1:3). By the tenth day of the first month of the following year (the forty-first of wandering), or seventy days later, the Israelites had only just crossed Jordan (cf. Josh. 4:19). In the last chapter of Deuteronomy we are told that they mourned Moses thirty days. Thus, the declaration of "this law" (1:5), or the entire book up to 34:8, covers less than forty days, although the review of Israel's wilderness experience included in it ranges over approximately forty years.

II. THE PURPOSE

There is no advance on the history of Israel, but rather a historical summary, in the form of discourses or exhortations, showing the true meaning and potentialities of all that had gone before. The new generation was on the border of Canaan and needed moral preparation for its future and for the planting of the true religion there. Thus, the book records the completion of God's training of His people for their life under the Theocracy. Note the following phrases as expressive of this divine purpose: "the land" (over 100 times); "given" — denoting bestowal of divine grace (75 times); "this day" (70 times); "possess" (nearly 70 times).

III. THE CONTENTS

1. Retrospect of Pathway (1:1 to 4:43)
 a. Introduction (1:1-5)
 b. Address of Moses (1:6 to 4:40)

 (1) Review (1:6 to 3:29)
 (a) Horeb to Kadesh-Barnea (chap. 1)
 (b) Kadesh-Barnea to Heshbon (chap. 2)
 (c) Heshbon to Beth-Peor (chap. 3)
 (2) Exhortation (4:1-40)
 c. Instructions regarding Cities of Refuge (4:41-43)

2. Resumé of Law (4:44 to 26:19)
 a. Introduction (4:44-49)
 b. Address of Moses (5:1 to 26:19)
 (1) General: Entry into the Land (chaps. 5 to 11)
 (a) Rehearsal of Decalogue as basis (chaps. 5, 6)
 (b) Application of First Table to Idolatry — Laws of Spiritual Life (chaps. 7 to 11)
 (2) Special: In the Land (chaps. 12 to 26)
 (a) Laws of Religious Life — Worship (12:1 to 16:17)
 (b) Laws of Political Life (16:18 to 20:19)
 (c) Laws of Social Life (chaps. 21 to 26)

3. Re-emphasis on Responsibility (chaps. 27 to 30)
 a. Series of Alternatives
 (1) Blessing and Cursing
 (2) Obedience and Disobedience
 (3) Life and Death
 b. Prospectvie — Future in the Land

4. Reminder of National Duty (chaps. 31 to 34)
 a. The Outlook (chap. 31)
 b. The Song (chap. 32)
 c. The Blessing (chap. 33)
 d. The End (chap. 34)

IV. THE CHARACTER

1. The exhortations in Deuteronomy fit the historical situation exactly. They were needed by the nation on the verge of its

Promised Land, for they contained not only review of the past, but also prophecy of the future with the alternative consequences of both loyalty to the worship of God and idolatry. This prophetic strain had been heard before when the Covenant was concerned (cf. Exod. 19:23; chap. 34; and Lev. 26). Knowing about the idolatry of Canaan, Moses warned and pledged Israel afresh.

2. The historical situation in Deuteronomy also accounts for the characteristics of the legislation, especially in view of the forty years of neglect and abeyance. Forty years for eleven days' journey! "Slow travellers because slow learners!" The immediate future was now in view and so there was need of union with God.

3. Deuteronomy is no mere repetition of Exodus and Leviticus, because the situation and purpose were different. There are no laws in Duteronomy for the desert, and we find some variation from Leviticus; e.g., cf. Leviticus 17:15 with Deuteronomy 14:21. The former allowed some laxity because the people were where animal food was scarce. Cf. also Leviticus 17:2 with Deuteronomy 12:15 for the laws of slaughter in the desert and in Canaan. There are few ritual laws in Deuteronomy, moreover, because this book was addressed to the people as a whole, while Leviticus was particularly for the priests.

4. We may notice all through Deuteronomy how much more than simply a review it is. It is also a means of preparation. In Exodus and Numbers the people were passing through these experiences, but in Deuteronomy they are looking back over them and drawing lessons from them. Therefore Moses gives many additions and explanations that are not found at all in Numbers. For example, regarding the appointment of the elders to assist Moses, in Numbers we are told that it was done, but we hear nothing of the instructions that Moses gave these judges. They are, however, given here (Deut. 1:16, 17). Again, in Numbers we are told that the spies were sent from Kadesh-Barnea, but it is not until we come to Deuteronomy 1:19-23 that we hear of the request coming from the people. Further, we are told in Numbers that Moses was forbidden to enter Canaan; but we hear nothing of the conversation between him and God until we come to Deuteronomy 3:23-28.

5. In Leviticus the sons of Aaron were distinguished from the Levites, and all instructions concerning them were separated and

detailed, while Deuteronomy uses the comprehensive term, "the priests the Levites." Yet a distinction comes out here also (cf. 10:6; 18:1; 33:8), and the dues to be paid by the people to the priests are mentioned in 18:3.

6. The laws regarding cleanness in Leviticus and regarding legal processes in Deuteronomy have one purpose, namely, to keep the people free from the contamination of the heathen. So also a central sanctuary is emphasized in the interest of unity and, therefore, of purity of worship.

7. These instances show why Deuteronomy differs from the rest of the Pentateuch, and close study shows its incompleteness by itself and consequent need of the preceding books. Thus it presupposes them: e.g., cf. 24:8 with Leviticus 13 and 14; 18:2 with Numbers 18:20, 23; 10:1 and 31:14 with former descriptions of the Ark and the Tabernacle; and 24:9 with the mention of Miriam in Numbers 12.

8. The style of Deuteronomy is so well marked as to point to its unity. Particular words and phrases recur and give distinctive coloring to every part of the book.

V. THE MESSAGE

The key-text is 6:3, with the main thought of Obedience. Numbers brings the people to the border of the Land; Deuteronomy prepares them to enter it and emphasizes —

1. The Necessity of Obedience: The Law of God.

Note the progress in the Pentateuch as a whole: Genesis gives the Choice of the People; Exodus, their Redemption; Leviticus, their Worship; Numbers, their Wanderings; Deuteronomy, their Obedience. While, therefore, Salvation is of grace, yet for enjoyment and testimony Obedience is essential. It is the call of the past, the duty of the present, and the guarantee of the future.

2. The Motive to Obedience: The Goodness of God.

Obedience is based on relationship, and relationship in this case on redemption (cf. "therefore," Rom. 12:1) :

> *I will not work my soul to save,*
> *For that my Lord has done;*
> *But I will work like any slave*
> *For love of God's dear Son.*

3. The Standard of Obedience: The Word of God.

This is the only standard, and yet it is wholly adequate. In chapter 6 there is a call to study it, and then a call to obey it.

4. The Incentive to Obedience: The Faithfulness of God.

This is the bed-rock of the divine revelation. As God was faithful in the past, so He will be in the future (cf. 1 Thess. 5:23, 24).

5. The Alternative to Obedience: The Justice of God.

He must administer punishment if His people are unfaithful and disobedient. Note the force of the word "if" in 28:2, 15; so also all through the New Testament.

CHAPTER STUDIES

Deuteronomy 1

Verses 1-5: General introduction, giving author, contents, and circumstances of place and time. The precise statements clearly involve Mosaic authorship and date.

Verse 6: First address of Moses, extending to 4:40, mainly retrospective of the forty years.

Verses 6-8: God's call to leave Sinai and the renewal of the promise concerning Canaan.

Verses 9-18: The great increase of Israel (Gen. 15:5) and the consequent inability of Moses to deal with every question. See Exodus 18:13-18 and Numbers 11:14. But the two are to be distinguished. The cause was the same (Moses' burdens), but the time and circumstances were quite different.

Verses 19-28: The story of the spies supplementing Numbers 13, showing that the suggestion came originally from the people.

Verses 29-40: The unsuccessful efforts of Moses to reassure the people.

Verses 41-46: The presumption of the people and their punishment.

THE MESSAGE FOR MEDITATION

(1) The beautiful picture of an old servant of God: his loving and large heart (v. 11); his absolute rightness (v. 17); his noble confidence (vv. 29, 30); his perfect frankness (v. 32). See Proverbs 16:31. (2) The sad consequences of unbelief and wilfulness — forty years when "eleven days" (v. 2) were all that was

necessary. (3) The patience of God with His people (vv. 10, 25, 26, 32).

Deuteronomy 2

THE NEW START from Kadesh and the journey to the border of Gilead.

Verse 1: "We" instead of "ye" (1:46) because narration not exhortation. "Many days" meant thirty-eight years.

Verses 2-8: From Kadesh to Seir. God's instructions and their reasons (vv. 4, 5).

Verse 9: Israel's relation to Moab.

Verses 10-12: A parenthetical account of former inhabitants of Moab.

Verses 13-16: Connected with verse 9, "Now rise up" are God's words, not Moses'! Zered was on the border, below Edom and Moab.

Verses 17-19: Instructions as to Ammon.

Verses 20-23: Second parenthesis, as verses 10-12.

Verses 24-37: Opposition of and victory over Sihon.

THE MESSAGE FOR MEDITATION

(1) God's perfect righteousness in protecting national rights (vv. 5, 9, 17). (2) God's definite requirement of strict obedience from His people (vv. 3, 37). (3) God's special care in preserving His children (v. 7): God's blessing, knowledge, presence, protection. (4) God's distinct influence on behalf of His people: fear (v. 25); deliverance (v. 33). And so comes the twofold relation (v. 3), God's to us, "I have begun to give," and ours to God, "begin to possess."

Deuteronomy 3

CONTINUATION of the Review of the Wilderness Experiences.

Verses 1-11: The conquest of Og, king of Bashan. This was on the east of Jordan, and took place before the people crossed that river (Num. 21:33-35). Bashan was formerly occupied by giants (Gen. 14:5), of whom Og alone remained (v. 11).

Verses 12-17: Distribution of the territory among the two and a half tribes.

Verses 18-20: The conditions of their possession. This narrative supplements the former (Num. 32:20-32).

Verses 21, 22: Joshua recognized as leader, instructed and encouraged.

Verses 23-29: The prayer of Moses (Num. 27:12-17). Verse 29 closes the review and so states the definite locality reached.

THE MESSAGE FOR MEDITATION

Pictures of God. (1) His encouragement of His people (vv. 2, 22, 28). (2) His relationship to His people, "our" (v. 3), "your" (vv. 18, 20, 21). (3) His power for His people, "I have given" (v. 18). (4) His will for His people (v. 26). "Does God always answer prayer?" "Yes," said a child, "sometimes He says 'Yes' and sometimes 'No.' "

Deuteronomy 4

EXHORTATIONS Based on the Preceding View of the History.

Verses 1-8: Obedience required. Two commands (hearken and do); three consequences (live, go in, possess). Reminders of the past point the exhortations.

Verses 9-14: Warning based especially on God's revelation of Himself.

Verses 15-20: Warnings based on the perils of idolatry.

Verses 21-24: Warning based on the divine nature.

Verses 25-31: Enforcement by the possibility of future disasters.

Verses 32-40: Enforcement through emphasis on God's special purpose.

Verses 41-43: The three cities of refuge. A picture of mercy and grace in the midst of insistence on obedience.

Verses 44-49: A general introduction to the next section: v. 45, three different words, all used with precision to describe different kinds of laws.

THE MESSAGE FOR MEDITATION

Pictures of Israel. (1) Israel's experience of loyalty to God (v. 4). (2) Israel's uniqueness as the people of God (vv. 6-8, 32-35). (3) Israel's need of faithfulness to God (vv. 9, 23, 40). (4) Israel's suffering through disobedience to God (vv. 25-30). (5) Israel's safety due to heeding the word of God (vv. 1, 2, 5, 6, 10, 13, 15, 30, 36, 40).

Deuteronomy 5

MOSES' SECOND ADDRESS, Extending to the End of Chapter 26. Chapter 4, verses 44 to 49 are an introduction referring to its general subject, the Law.

Verses 1-5: The circumstances of the giving of the Decalogue. The basis was a covenant, which is to be carefully distinguished from the Abrahamic Covenant (Gen. 15).

Verses 6-21: The Decalogue. The differences between this and Exodus 20 shows that Deuteronomy is no mere repetition, but has special points of its own which should be noted in all references to the past. The main difference is in the reason for Sabbath observance. Exodus 20 is general, referring to all men; Deuteronomy 5 is special, applying particularly to Israel. The two are thus complementary.

Verses 22-27: The attitude of the people. Special emphasis on the "fire" or symbol of God's presence. Elaboration of Exodus 20:15-18.

Verses 28-33: The divine response and recognition. Not given in Exodus.

THE MESSAGE FOR MEDITATION

(1) The order of the Christian life: redemption, relationship (v. 5) and righteousness (6:25). (2) The obligation of the Christian life. Based on the divine character (vv. 4, 5, 22-26). (3) The outcome of the Christian life. Obedience covering thoughts, words, and deeds in relation to God (vv. 7-16) and man (vv. 17-21).

Deuteronomy 6

CONTINUATION of Appeal, But a New Section.

Verses 1-3: General preface to what follows. The purpose and results of obedience.

Verses 4, 5: The great commandment. The unity of the God-head as the basis of unity of purpose in us.

Verses 6-9: The witness of the truth to others: "teach," "talk," "sign," "frontlets," "write."

Verses 10-19: Warnings about Canaan. Three perils (vv. 12, 14, 16).

Verses 20-25: The children's inquiry and the parental response. Elaboration of verse 7.

THE MESSAGE FOR MEDITATION

(1) The purpose of life (vv. 1-3, 24) : "do"; "possess"; "fear"; "keep"; "well"; "increase"; "our good"; "preserve." (2) The principle of life (v. 4) : love, the basis of loyalty. (3) The plan of life (vv. 6-10) : from the heart outward to home and country. (4) The peril of life: "lest thou forget" (v. 12).

Deuteronomy 7

Verses 1-5: Call to Separation. The reason was idolatry (v. 4). Three features: complete extermination (v. 2) ; personal separation (v. 3) ; religious intolerance (v. 5). (See Exod. 23:32; 34:12-16; Lev. 27:28).

Verses 6-8: The reasons for this attitude of separateness.

Verses 9-11 : God's own attitude as the basis. This is twofold: "love" (v. 9) ; "hate" (v. 10).

Verses 12-15: God's promises. Obedience brings blessing.

Verses 16-21 : Fears assured.

Verses 22-26: Victory gradual but certain. Renewed emphasis on separateness.

THE MESSAGE FOR MEDITATION

(1) An absolute necessity, separation. The great principle of Scripture from Genesis 4. (See 2 Cor. 6:17). (2) A unique position (vv. 6-8), chosen of God. (3) A great promise, victory. (4) A blessed assurance (v. 18), not afraid. (5) A significant reminder (v. 22), "little and little."

Deuteronomy 8

Verses 1-4: An appeal to memory. Keyword, "remember" (v. 2). Note "all" (v. 1) ; "all" (v. 2) ; "every word" (v. 3).

Verses 5-10: An appeal to experience. Keyword, "consider" (v. 5).

Verses 11-20: An appeal to anticipation. Keyword, "beware" (v. 11).

THE MESSAGE FOR MEDITATION

(1) Discipleship is associated with discipline (vv. 2, 3). (2) Discipline is meant for spiritual profit (vv. 4, 5; Heb. 12:5-13).

(3) Profit is accompanied by blessing (vv. 7-9). (4) Blessing should be marked by recognition of God (vv. 10-20).

Deuteronomy 9

Verses 1-6: The true attitude of trust in God and self. Warning against self-righteousness and emphasis on divine power and faithfulness.

Verses 7-24: Reminder of past failures: at Sinai (vv. 7-21); elsewhere (vv. 22-24). Compare Exodus 32. The sinfulness was "chronic" (v. 24).

Verses 25-29: Moses' intercession at Sinai.

The Message for Meditation

(1) The place of memory in religion (v. 7). (2) The peril of emotion (without principle) in religion (v. 12). (3) The proof of reality in religion (persistent loyalty). (4) The power of interecession in religion (v. 26).

Deuteronomy 10

Verses 1-11: Results of Moses' intercession. Compare Exodus 33 and 34. (1) Renewal of covenant (vv. 1-5); (2) provision for worship (vv. 6-10); (3) restoration of favor (v. 11).

Verses 12-22: Appeal based on God's goodness: (1) obedience (vv. 12, 13); (2) purity (v. 16); (3) love to others (v. 19); (4) loyalty (v. 20).

The Message for Meditation

(1) The requirements of God indicated. (2) The revelation of God described (vv. 12, 13, 14, 17, 18, 20, 21). (3) The religion of God summarized (vv. 20-22) fear, serve, cleave, swear by His name, thy praise.

Deuteronomy 11

This chapter closes the general appeal based on the Decalogue (see Outline in Introduction).

Verses 1-7: Obedience based on God's wonderful work in the past. Verse 6, see Numbers 16:31-33. Korah is not mentioned. Is this because his sons were still alive, not being destroyed with their father?

Verses 8-12: Obedience based on God's favor in the future.

Verse 8: Strength as the outcome of faithfulness to God.

Verse 9: Contrast between Egypt and Canaan, as between human resources and divine blessing. Egypt was rainless and dependent upon man's effort; Canaan was well watered from heaven, and suggested God's favor (Psa. 65:9-13).

Verse 10: "Foot," probably referring to water wheels which were worked by the feet. The allusion is to toilsomeness.

Verses 13-17: Blessings accruing from obedience and their opposites.

Verse 14: First or former rain fell from October to December, preparing the land for seed. The latter rain came in March and April, while grain, etc., was ripening.

Verses 18-25: Personal, domestic, and social faithfulness and its results.

Verse 24: See Joshua 1:3. The "uttermost" is "hinder" or "western" sea (Mediterranean), that which was behind when one faced the East. Verses 21-25 give a wonderful account of what God would do.

Verses 26-32: Alternatives. Ebal and Gerizim were in the center of the land (v. 30). "Champaign" is the Arabah or plain in the South. "Plains" should be "oaks" (Gen. 12:6).

Verse 32 is the concluding summary of chaps. 5-11.

THE MESSAGE FOR MEDITATION

(1) The Summary of true life (vv. 1, 13, 22): love and obedience. (2) The contrast between our eyes (v. 7) and God's (v. 12). (3) The Word of God our constant guide and guard (vv. 1, 8, 13, 18-20, 22, 27, 32). (4) The emphasis on the grace of God as against human endeavor and toil (cf. Eph. 2:1-10).

Deuteronomy 12

AT THIS POINT begins (see Outline in Introduction) the inculcation of special laws (chaps. 12 to 26), which Israel was to obey in Canaan. After obedience as a principle (chaps. 5 to 11), come various applications.

Verses 1-3: Destruction of the sacred shrines of idolatry.

Verse 2: Heathenism used hills and mountains, apparently because they were thought nearer to the gods worshipped.

Verses 4-14: The place of worship of Jehovah, limited to one particular spot, as against heathenism with its self-assertion (worshipping anywhere). This restriction would be a constant reminder of God's separateness and authority. The absence of the name of the place is a signal proof of the early date of Deuteronomy. Jerusalem is not named in the Pentateuch, for the obvious reason that its selection as the central place for worship was made ages after the time of Moses (2 Sam. 6:12).

Verse 6: Four groups of offerings.

Verse 12: Because the Levites had no inheritance and were therefore to be dispersed over Canaan (Num. 35).

Verses 15-28: Home needs and religious requirements (Lev. 17:3). Distinction between ordinary food and religious gifts. The exception was the avoidance of blood (Gen. 9:4; Lev. 7:26).

Verses 29-32: Reception of warning against idolatry.

The Message for Meditation

(1) The impossibility of compromise in religion (vv. 1-3). (2) The one and only place for meeting God (vv. 5, 11, 14, 18, 21, 26). Christ the only way (John 14:6; Acts 4:12). (3) The various offerings as symbolic of entire consecration (Rom. 12:1). (4) The attitude of the soul, "before the Lord" (vv. 7, 12; 14:26; 16: 11, 14; 26:11; 27:7). See Leviticus 23:40 and Genesis 17:1.

Deuteronomy 13

One topic only, but in three aspects, adherence to the one true God.

Verses 1-5: Temptation through a false prophet. The false prophet is quite prominent in the Old Testament. Even miracles cannot set aside truth. What the prophet *did* was wonderful, but what he *said* was wrong (see 2 Thess. 2:8-12; 1 John 4:1; 2 John 10, 11).

Verses 6-11. Temptation through our own kin. No thought of affection to prevent severe dealing. For the principle, see Luke 14:26.

Verses 12-18: Action against unfaithfulness.

THE MESSAGE FOR MEDITATION

(1) The Christian's general conduct as suggested by the word "walk," sincerity, "before" (Gen. 17:1); obedience, "after" (Deut. 13:4); union, "in" (Col. 2:6); fellowship, "with" (Gen. 5:24). (2) The specific features here emphasized: watchfulness enjoined (vv. 1-5); faithfulness urged (vv. 6-11); righteousness emphasized (vv. 12-18).

Deuteronomy 14

FURTHER marks of the people of God.

Verses 1, 2: No physical lacerations or other indications of mourning (Lev. 19:28; Jer. 16:6; Ezek. 7:18).

Verses 3-20: Permissions and prohibitions as to food, animals (vv. 3-8); fish (vv. 9, 10); birds (vv. 11-20). The "pygarg" (v. 5 KJV) was probably a species of antelope, and the "glede" (v. 13 KJV) found only here, is thought to have been a bird of the hawk type, perhaps a buzzard or kite.

Verse 21: Two special prohibitions. For the latter, see Exodus 23:19; 34:26. The stranger was free from these restrictions because he was not in covenant with God.

Verses 22-29: Tithes and offerings (vv. 28, 29) refer to the same tithes put to a different use.

THE MESSAGE FOR MEDITATION

(1) The attitude of the believer — separation (vv. 1-21). (2) The reason for the attitude — "children" (v. 1) — "holy" (v. 21). (3) The outcome of the attitude — blessing (v. 29).

Deuteronomy 15

Verses 1-6: Release of debtors. The "Lord's release" (v. 2) is the Sabbatical year, and this was a provision whereby every Jew would enjoy its privileges. It does not seem to mean entire remission of debt but only a postponement until the Sabbatical year was over, because the land would not then be under cultivation. Foreigners (v. 3) were not included in this law (v. 4). "Save only" (KJV) should be "Howbeit," meaning that it was to prevent poverty.

Verses 7-11: Philanthropy to the needy. A call to large-hearted unselfishness.

Verses 12-18: Emancipation of slaves (Exod. 21:2-6).

Verses 13, 14 are an addition to the former law, ordering provision to be made for the slave to begin a house of his own.

Verses 19-23: Sanctification of the first-born animals, see Exodus 13.

THE MESSAGE FOR MEDITATION

(1) The reality of true life seen in (a) loyalty to God, (b) love to man, (c) liberality to the needy. (2) The reason for true life seen in (a) God's future blessing (vv. 4-6, 10); (b) God's present blessing (v. 7); (c) God's past blessing (vv. 14, 15).   See Philippians 2:1-8; Galatians 6:1-10. "Ye are not your own;" "Them that honour Me, I will honour."

Deuteronomy 16

THE THREE chief feasts.

The fuller instructions in Leviticus 23 were for the priests; these briefer ones were especially adapted for the people.

Verses 1-8: The Passover (Exod. 12:2; 23:15). Again the special "place" is mentioned; Christ's Death was the antitype (1 Cor. 5:7).

Verses 9-12: The Feast of Weeks, or Pentecost. Mark the joy (v. 11) in contrast to the affliction (v. 3). The Resurrection and the Day of Pentecost form the antitype.

Verses 13-15: Feast of Tabernacles (Exod. 23:17; 34:33). No antitype to this has yet occurred; it is still future (see below).

Verses 16, 17: The yearly appearance and accompaniment of gifts. Proportionate giving, "as he is able;" "according to the blessing."

Verses 18-20: The appointment, character, and work of judges.

Verses 21, 22: The vital peril of idolatry. "Grove" is incorrect; it is "Asherah," a wooden idol, symbolical of the goddess Astarte. (KJV) "Plant" refers to the fixing of the idol in the ground.

THE MESSAGE FOR MEDITATION

(1) The Three Feasts: Passover, suggesting our *pardon* through Christ's Death; Pentecost, symbolizing our *provision* through Christ's Resurrection; Tabernacles, foreshadowing our *prospect* through Christ's Coming. (2) The Three Attitudes: thankfulness for past deliverance, joy in present grace, hope in future glory.

Deuteronomy 17

Verse 1: Sacrifices to be unblemished. A safeguard against profanation (Lev. 22:19-24).

Verses 2-7: Punishment for apostasy. In chapter 13 reference is to those who lead others into idolatry. Here, it is to those who are led. The "gates" were places of judicial proceedings in the East (v. 8). The emphasis is on "evil" (vv. 1, 7). In verses 6, 7, the requirement is made of adequate evidence (Num. 35:30).

Verses 8-13: The appeal for judicial decisions (Exod. 18: 19-26). In verse 9, the supreme tribunal. The phrase "the priests the Levites" is characteristic of Deuteronomy, and means "the priests who were of the tribe of Levi." In verse 12, presumptuous sin had no sacrifice (Num. 15:30).

Verses 14-20: The monarchy anticipated. Likeness (v. 14) and yet unlikeness (vv. 16-20) to other nations. In verse 18, "copy" means "double" or "duplicate," whence comes the Greek title, Deuteronomy, "Second Law" or repetition. But the Book is much more than this.

THE MESSAGE FOR MEDITATION

Some necessities. (1) Our best for God (v. 1). (2) Righteousness in heart and life (vv. 1-7). (3) Justice in relation to others (vv. 8-13). (4) Submission to God (vv. 10-13). (5) Loyalty to God's Word (vv. 18, 19).

Deuteronomy 18

Verses 1-5: The maintenance of the priests (Num. 18, 20, 23, 24).

Verse 3 refers to choice parts.

Verses 6-8: The Levites.

Verses 9-14: Against idolatry in Canaan. The practices were all associated with false worship. "Perfect" (v. 13) means upright, sincere (Gen. 17:1).

Verses 15-19: The true prophet. No need for Israel to depend on diviners, because they would have a prophet of their own. The reference is, first, to a succession of prophets to meet the constant need against idolatry (vv. 9-14). Yet the singular, "prophet," indicates one prophet pre-eminent, and so the reference is ultimately to Christ (Acts 3:22). A prophet represented God to man

(Exod. 7:1), and a priest represented man to God (Heb. 5: 1).

Verses 20-22: The false prophet. Tested by fulfillment of prediction. See Isaiah 41:23. Chap. 13:2 gives the other test.

THE MESSAGE FOR MEDITATION

(1) Christ our priest, representing us to God by sacrifice and intercession (Heb. 5:5-9; 4:14). (2) Christ our prophet, representing God to us by the revelation of His truth and will.

Deuteronomy 19

Verses 1-3: The Cities of Refuge to be appointed in Canaan (Num. 35: 1-34; Deut. 4:41-49).

Verses 2, 3 give supplementary instructions. Every facility was to be afforded. The institution is unknown outside Israel, and so is a testimony to the justice and humaneness of the Mosaic code.

Verses 4-10: Conditions of using these cities.

Verses 8, 9 refer to three beyond the six, but the extra ones were never needed, because Israel's disobedience kept it from extending its boundaries.

Verse 10 is another reference to blood, emphasizing its sanctity.

Verses 11-13: Those for whom these cities were not intended. Not a shelter for murderers.

Verse 14: The sacred landmark. (See 27:17; Job 24:2; Prov. 22:28; 23:10; Hos. 5:10).

Verses 15-21: Adequate evidence and false testimony.

THE MESSAGE FOR MEDITATION

Three elements of the believer's life. (1) Refuge provided (vv. 1-10). (2) Reality emphasized (vv. 11-14). (3) Righteousness demanded (vv. 15-21).

Deuteronomy 20

SOME LAWS of warfare. Found in this book only.

Verses 1-9: Encouragement in face of an enemy with greater resources. In verse 2, apparently the priest was appointed to accompany the army.

Verses 5-7: The priest is first mentioned in connection with God's promises and assurances. Then the officers (v. 5) are referred to in connection with requirements and responsibilities. The men exempted from military service.

Verse 8: Significant treatment of the timid, and the reason for his exemption.

Verses 10-20: The siege of a city. (1) Invitation to surrender (v. 10). (2) Action on refusal (v. 14). This applied only to cities at a distance (v. 15), not to those of the Canaanites, which did not come under this rule (Exod. 23:31-33; 34:11-16).

THE MESSAGE FOR MEDITATION

A fivefold view of God. (1) God's promise in case of danger (vv. 1-4). (2) God's provision in the face of emergencies (vv. 6, 7; 2 Tim. 2:4). (3) God's peace in view of surrender (vv. 10, 11). (4) God's power in the midst of opposition (vv. 12-18). (5) God's principle in the presence of opportunity (vv. 19, 20), "that nothing be lost."

Deuteronomy 21

VARIOUS REGULATIONS.

Verses 1-9: Unknown murder and its expiation.

Verse 2: "Elders," leaders of the people, "judges," legal administrators.

Verse 4:"Rough" (KJV) means "through which a stream flows," the blood being carried away by the water.

Verses 6, 7: Symbolical declaration of innocence.

Verses 10-14: Captive women. This would not apply to a Canaanitish woman, with whom no such alliance was permitted (7:3).

Verse 12: Signs of symbolical purification, preparatory to separation from heathenism and entrance into God's covenant with Israel.

Verses 15-17: Justice to the first-born.

Verse 17: "Double," mark of the birthright (2 Kings 2:9).

Verses 18-21: A rebellious son. Emphasis on obedience to parents as the foundation of social and national life. This national feature is in contrast with the purely personal attitude of the father to the prodigal (Luke 15).

Verses 22, 23: Exposure and burial of the corpse of a criminal.

Verse 22 is not an execution, but exposure after death.

Verse 23: "Accursed" is under God's ban or condemnation. The exposure is regarded as defiling the land (Lev. 18:24, 25). Note the illustration afforded by Christ's death (Gal. 3:13).

THE MESSAGE FOR MEDITATION

(1) The constant reminder of sin and the need of expiation, even of unknown wrongdoing (vv. 1-9, 22, 23). (2) The perpetual emphasis of the necessity of righteousness in heart and life (vv. 15-21).

Deuteronomy 22

NO CLASSIFICATION is possible of these separate requirements.

Verses 1-4: Duty of brotherhood in regard to loss. Repetition and elaboration of Exodus 23: 4, 5.

Verse 5: Distinction between the sexes. "Abomination," because of the possibility of evil.

Verses 6, 7: Humanity and parental affection.

Verse 8: Protection of life, due to flat roofs in the East which needed balustrades.

Verses 9-11: Distinctions in nature to be observed (Lev. 19: 19). Some say the wrong was due to the connection with idolatry, not the mere wearing, but the particular shape with superstitious associations. So with the seeds, "it was a superstitious custom of the idolaters" (see Zeph. 1:8).

Verse 12: "Fringes" were "tassels" (Num. 15:38) at each of the four corners of the robe (Matt. 9:20). The meaning is obscure. Some suggest it was for the purpose of aiding the memory, or else for propriety in some way.

Verses 13-29: Laws of personal purity. Four cases distinguished: 22; 23; 24; 25-27; 28, 29.

Verse 30: The supreme form of wrong (Lev. 18:7).

THE MESSAGE FOR MEDITATION

(1) The necessity and importance of little things in character and condition. "Perfection is made up of trifles and perfection is no trifle." Small points in life are the best test of reality. (2) Features of true life: brotherliness (vv. 1-4); kindness to animals (v. 4); purity (vv. 5, 13-30); humanity (vv. 6, 7); considerateness (v. 8); naturalness (vv. 9-11); genuineness (v. 11).

Deuteronomy 23

Verses 1-8: Exclusion from the congregation — five classes, but the last two may be received at the third generation. Does this mean membership in the Israelitish community? Or only the holding of office? (Exod. 12:48, 49). "Tenth" may be literal, indicative of caution and especially because it would protect Israel against marriages with these nations. Or it may mean permanent exclusion ("forever," v. 6), "tenth" being used for indefiniteness, as in Genesis 31:7 and Numbers 14:22.

Verses 9:14: Regulations against physical impurity.

Verse 13, "paddle" (KJV) is "spade," which was to be connected with military weapons.

Verses 15, 16: An escaped foreign slave was not to be surrendered, but allowed freedom. Israel would thus be a refuge against oppression.

Verses 17, 18: This was because of idolatry, which was invariably associated with sensuality (Mic. 1:7). "Dog" is a man, a male devotee of evil, "dog" being a synonym for anything unclean.

Verses 19-25: Personal rights and duties: usury (vv. 19, 20); vows (vv. 21-23); "for necessity, not for superfluity" (vv. 24, 25).

THE MESSAGE FOR MEDITATION

God in relation to us (v. 14). (1) Possession, "thy." (2) Presence, "midst." (3) Progress, "walketh." (4) Power, "deliver." (5) Purity, "holy."

Deuteronomy 24

Verses 1-4: Divorce.

Verse 5: Exemption of the newly-married from military service for one year (20:7).

Verse 6: To pawn one stone would be to deprive the owner of the means of preparing food.

Verse 7: Exodus 21:16.

Verses 8, 9: Leprosy (Lev. 13 and 14). For Miriam (Num. 12:14).

Verses 10-13: Pledges.

Verses 14, 15: Justice to laborers.

Verse 16: Personal responsibility. Earthly authorities might not do this but God could (Exod. 20:5).

Verses 17, 18: Justice to three classes of the needy (Exod. 22: 20, 21; 23:9).

Verses 19-22: Positive kindness, not mere negative avoidance of wrong and injustice.

THE MESSAGE FOR MEDITATION

(1) Memory of past blessing an incentive to present faithfulness (vv. 9, 18, 22). (2) Purity in every relation of life (vv. 4. 7, 8). (3) Kindness to the helpless and the needy (vv. 6, 7, 10, 11, 14, 15, 19, 21).

Deuteronomy 25

FURTHER LIST of various regulations.

Verses 1-3: Corporal punishment and its limits.

Verse 4: Rights of animals in service. (Note the use made of this verse in Matt. 10:9-11; Luke 10:7; I Cor. 9:9, 10; 1 Tim. 5: 17, 18).

Verses 5-10: Levirate marriages. Their purpose was to preserve families from extinction and property from passing to strangers. They were based on what was regarded as family honor, childlessness being considered a disgrace. This will also explain verses 7-10, and the indignity and ignominy meted out to refusal.

Verses 11, 12: Severe punishment for exceptional sin.

Verses 13-16: Strict justice in business.

Verses 17-19: Judgment against Israel's inveterate foe. The contrast between this and the kindness among themselves as seen in earlier verses is notable.

THE MESSAGE FOR MEDITATION

Further emphasis on daily life and its characteristics. (1) Humanity in punishment (vv. 1-3). (2) Righteousness in business (vv. 4, 13-16). (3) Severity against evil (vv. 11, 12, 17-19).

Deuteronomy 26

THE SECOND ADDRESS of Moses closes here, as it began (chap. 12) with a reference to the Tabernacle or central place of worship.

Verses 1-11: The first fruits (Num. 18:12).

Verse 5: The "Syrian" is Jacob.

Verse 11: A joyous meal was to crown everything.

Verses 12-15. The tithes. (To be carefully distinguished from the annual tithe of Lev. 27:30-33 and Num. 18:21-32). Every third year the tithe was to be given to the poor.

Verse 13: Sincerity before God.

Verse 14: "Mourning," the time during which the man was ceremoniously impure. "Dead," either (1) had not given any part to those who mourn the dead (2 Sam. 3:35), or (2) had not helped by gift anyone involved in death, *i.e.*, had not diverted possessions to any other use, even the most urgent — death.

Verses 16-19: A solemn appeal for obedience. "Avouch" (KJV) declare.

Verse 18: "Peculiar," especially (peculiarly) God's own possession. (Latin, *peculium;* Titus 2:14).

THE MESSAGE FOR MEDITATION

(1) Remembrance of God (v. 5). (2) Recognition of God (v. 10). (3) Resolve to God (v. 17). Note the exchange of solemn pledges (vv. 17, 18): ours to God, fourfold (v. 17): possession, conduct, faithfulness, and attention. God's to us, fourfold: possession, purpose, position, purity.

Deuteronomy 27

MOSES' THIRD ADDRESS covers chapters 27-30.

Verses 1-8: The testimony to be borne in Canaan. Pillars were to be set up and the law was to be inscribed on them. The number of stones is not mentioned, but as the entire legislative portions were to be put on them, several would be needed. "Plaister" (v. 2) was probably "a coating of lime or gypsum." An altar also was to be erected (vv. 5-7).

Verses 9, 10: Fresh appeal for obedience.

Verses 11-14: The pronouncement of the blessings on Mount Gerizim, and the curses on Mount Ebal (11:29).

Verses 15-26: Twelve curses (the number of the tribes). The blessings are not recorded, but they were included in the fulfilment of this requirement (Josh. 8:34). The blessings of chapter 28 are quite different. It is known from travellers that the voice could carry far enough for all to hear. Each of the first eleven curses refers to some particular sin against God's law (see references in Bible). The twelfth is general, covering the entire law. For the contrast between law and grace, see Galatians 3:13 and Romans 8:1.

THE MESSAGE FOR MEDITATION

Elements of a godly life. (1) Testimony to God's law (vv. 1-3). (2) Consecration of life, "burnt offering" (v. 6). (3) Fellowship with God, "peace offerings" (v. 7). (4) Obedience because of privilege, "therefore" (v. 10). (5) Blessing (v. 12). (6) Judgment on sin (vv. 13-26). (7) Acceptance of position. "Amen" is not a prayer, but a response of endorsement.

Deuteronomy 28

THE SOLEMN CONTRASTS of blessings and curses. The reference is to Israel as a nation in the light of God's purpose (Exod. 19:6).

Verses 1-14: Blessings, based on obedience (vv. 1, 2): in personal life, eight aspects (vv. 3-7); in home and city (vv. 8-14).

Verses 15-68: Curses. Due to disobedience (v. 15); in personal life, eight aspects (vv. 16-19). Sequence is not easy to see. It has been suggested that there are five groups: verses 15-19; verses 20-26; verses 27-34; verses 35-46; verses 58-68. "Botch (KJV) of Egypt" (v. 27) is probably the leprosy found in Egypt; so also verse 35, leprosy. The curses develop into predictions (vv. 49-68), which Jewish history shows to have been fulfilled.

Verse 60: "Diseases" are the plagues, and verse 68 may be typical or literal. The latter was true of the Jewish slaves carried into Egypt after the capture of Jerusalem, A.D. 70.

THE MESSAGE FOR MEDITATION

The simple but certain contrasts of life. (1) The results of obedience ("happy" John 13:17). (2) The consequences of disobedience. (3) The two services (vv. 47, 48). (4) The two joys (v. 63).

Deuteronomy 29

THE COVENANT MADE on the plains of Moab, just before entrance into Canaan.

Verses 1-9: Reminder. "Beside" (v. 1). Some think this was a ratification of the covenant at Sinai, especially because no sacrifices are found here and these are invariably associated with covenants. But it seems better to think of it as a special covenant made with particular reference to Canaan (vv. 12-14). See the Scofield Bible on chapter 30.

Verse 4: Disobedience always results in lack of insight (Isa. 6:9, 10).

Verses 10-15: Appeal. A national engagement, including children (v. 11) and strangers (vv. 11, 15).

Verses 16-29: Warning. Danger of apostasy.

Verse 19: "Add"(KJV) a proverbial expression for the culminating effect of wrong-doing.

Verse 23: Allusion to country around the Dead Sea. ,

THE MESSAGE FOR MEDITATION

Spiritual perils. (1) Lest we become blind (v. 4; Matt. 13:14, 15; 2 Cor. 3:14, 15; Eph. 4:18). (2) Lest we forget (v. 18). (3) Lest we presume (v. 19). (4) Lest we forsake (v. 25).

Deuteronomy 30

THE OUTLOOK EXTENDS to the future, as one of the "secret things" of 29:29.

Verses 1-10: Repentance. The result will be restoration (See Amos 9:11, 12; Rom. 11). The restoration of the Jews is clear from many Scriptures.

Verses 11-14: Return. Faithfulness to God is not difficult. In Romans 10:6-13, Paul uses this of the Christian position of grace. But this is no mere accommodation and application, for even to Israel, obedience to God's will was easy. Grace existed before law (Gen. 15:6; Psa. 32:1, 2). See Psalm 19:7-14.

Verses 15-20: Reminder. Alternatives stated with emphasis on the power of choice.

THE MESSAGE FOR MEDITATION

(1) A threefold call: repentance, trust, obedience. (2) A threefold blessing: restoration after repentance (vv. 1-10); opportunity for faith and faithfulness (vv. 11-14); life through obedience (vv. 15-19). (3) A threefold experience: cleaving, living, abiding.

Deuteronomy 31

HERE COMMENCE the closing scenes of Moses' life. His work as leader was practically done, and all that remained was to give some farewell counsels and warnings.

Verses 1-6: Last counsels to the people. For Moses' age (v. 2) see Exodus 7:7.

Verses 7, 8: Exhortation to Joshua. Mark the emphasis on courage (vv. 7-23; Joshua 1:5-9).

Verses 9-13: Instructions to the priests and elders. The Feast of Tabernacles would be an appropriate time for this, because of its association with the memory of deliverance from Egypt and consequent necessity of obedience.

Verses 14-23: The divine appearance, with commands and warnings. The song that is recorded in chapter 32.

Verses 24-27: Embodiment of law in book-form. A clear claim of Moses to the authorship of Deuteronomy. It was customary in the East to deposit the book of the law at the sanctuary.

Verses 28, 29: Closing precautions.

THE MESSAGE FOR MEDITATION

An old man's counsels as to the essentials of spiritual success. (1) Strength from God (v. 6). (2) Courage in God (vv. 6, 8). (3) Confidence in God (vv. 3, 6, 8). (4) Knowledge of the Word of God (vv. 11-13). (5) Faithfulness to the will of God (vv. 14-21, 29). (6) Adherence to the law of God (v. 26).

Deuteronomy 32

THE SONG OF MOSES was composed by God's command (31:19), recited to the people, and then put in writing (31:22). The theme is the contrast between God and the people, faithfulness with unfaithfulness, love and rebellion.

Verses 1-3: Introduction. The theme.

Verse 2: Suggests the power of the message.

Verses 4-6: God's way and the people's set in contrast.

Verses 7-18: God's work of redemption and the people's wilful ingratitude.

Verses 19-27: God's righteous punishment (v. 27), lest the enemy should ascribe his victory over Israel to his own power.

Verses 28-33: The explanation of Israel's sins is unwisdom and folly.

Verse 32: The vine is Israel, but it had become corrupt like Sodom.

Verses 34-43: God's judgments and mercies.

Verse 34: "This" seems to blend Israel's sin and God's punishment as "laid up," awaiting the proper time.

Verses 44-47: Moses' appeal based on the song.

Verses 48-52: The call to Moses in regard to his death. N.B. The chapter refers primarily to Israel, and can only be used by us in the Church of Christ with secondary spiritual application.

THE MESSAGE FOR MEDITATION

The Song is full of God, both in its plain statements and its metaphors. (1) The greatness of God (vv. 3-8). (2) The grace of God (vv. 9-14). In v. 10, four aspects of the spiritual life: "found," "led about," "instructed," "kept." (3) The faithfulness of God (vv. 15-18). (4) The judgment of God (vv. 19-27). (5) The power of God (vv. 30, 31). (6) The righteousness of God (vv. 35-42). (7) The mercy of God (v. 43).

Deuteronomy 33

THE BLESSING OF the tribes by Moses before ascending Nebo. The contrast to the song (chap. 32) which recounts the results of the people's sins, while this records the divine blessings. This should be compared with Jacob's blessings (Gen. 49). There are points of contact because the tribes are the same, while there are points of difference because the time and circumstances are different.

Verses 1-5: Introduction. Emphasis on God as the source of everything.

Verse 1: "Man of God," used of Moses in Joshua 14:6 and title of Psalm 90. The usual prophetic title of a man as God's servant and messenger.

Verse 2: "Fiery law," or rays of fire (Ex. 19:16; Hab. 3:4).

Verses 6-25: The blessings of the tribes.

Verse 6: Continuance.

Verse 7: Help.

Verses 8-11: Favor. Why is Simeon omitted? (Gen. 49:7). Is it because of his omission to help Levi in Exodus 32:26-29? Or because he tended to lose his tribal individuality? He is included in Judah in Joshua 19:2-9.

Verse 12: Protection.

Verses 13-17: Prosperity.

Verses 18, 19: Obedience.

Verses 20, 21: Strength.

Verse 22: Power.

Verse 23: Satisfaction.

Verses 24, 25: Sufficiency.

Verses 26-29: Summary description of God in relation to Israel.

THE MESSAGE FOR MEDITATION

A chapter of blessings. (1) The Incomparable ("like," v. 26) Source of blessing. God's light (v. 2), love (vv. 3, 12), power (vv. 3, 26, 27, 29), truth (v. 3). (2) The Incomparable ("like," v. 29) Character of blessing: Israel's power (vv. 7, 20-22), protection (vv. 6, 12), provision (vv. 13-17), prosperity (vv. 18, 19, 23).

Deuteronomy 34

THE CLOSING SCENES of Moses' life.

Verses 1-4: The view of Canaan. Moses was allowed to see, but not, for the present, could he enter. His prayer to enter Canaan was fulfilled at the Transfiguration.

Verse 5: The "servant" and "the word" were the two characteristics of his life. See "man of God" (33:1).

Verse 6: See Jude 9. This must have taken place soon after the burial.

Verse 7: His life had three periods of forty years each.

Verse 9: The new leader, his qualifications and recognition by the people.

Verses 10-12: The testimony to Moses.

THE MESSAGE FOR MEDITATION

The secrets of all true life. (1) Fellowship with God (v. 10). (2) Service for God (v. 11). (3) Testimony to God (v. 12).

8

A BRIEF REVIEW OF THE PENTATEUCH

I. GENERAL

1. The key to the unity of the Bible is the purpose of God for the redemption of the world. The story of its unfolding is in two parts: first, as it was confined to the Jewish nation; and second, as it was revealed to be intended for all mankind.

2. In the Old Testament there are thus two stages: first, the historical introduction of the Divine Religion into the world, and this, as we have seen, forms the Pentateuch; and second, the historical development of the Divine Religion in the world, recounted in the remainder of the Old Testament.

II. SPECIFIC

The Pentateuch's historical introduction is in five phases, each a distinct yet connected, an essential and natural part of an organic whole. They cover a very long period of time, from the Creation to the death of Moses:

1. Genesis. The origin of the Divine Religion and of the People who were to be its guardians.

2. Exodus. The committal of the Divine Religion to the Chosen People and the establishment of the Divine Presence among them.

3. Leviticus. The methods of approach to God for worship on the part of the People.

4. Numbers. The organization and discipline of the People for their work.

5. Deuteronomy. The preparation of the People for entering their Promised Land where the Divine Religion was to be established.

III. CRITICAL

This word is used, of course, in the primary sense of judging, evaluating:

1. It is clear from a close scrutiny of the five Books that there is one purpose throughout. The Pentateuch is a complete and connected account of the origin and development of Divine Redemption, and its unity of design presupposes a single author.

2. Not one of the five Books is complete in itself, nor free from reference to the others. We may compare particularly the first words of each and the historical threads running through all of them. The story of Redemption is continued and developed throughout, and the legislation contained therein is connected and progressive.

3. All the later Books of the Bible either imply the existence of the Pentateuch or else definitely refer to it.

4. Even though there obviously were pre-existing materials, differences in dates, and also three stages of the Levitical law, there is no necessity to separate the Books by centuries.

5. Genesis covers thousands of years; Exodus, 145 years; Numbers, 39 years; Leviticus, about 30 days; and Deuteronomy, 40 days. There was ample time for changes among the people of Israel from the period of Sinai to that of Jordan. Their laws needed modification through circumstances; this can be seen even in one Book (cf. Num. 4:1 and 8:24). The large amount of change in so short a time suggests an important historical crisis.

6. It is wise to credit the Pentateuch with honesty until it is proved to be fiction. It is not possible that later prophets or other writers made one code of laws, then another, then a third, and deliberately used great names (even God's) to represent history as different from what, through other sources, we know it actually was. It is strange that the very scholars who expound the theory that seventy years' exile later on made the marvellous transition in Israel from idolatry to purity of religion will not allow in forty years in the wilderness a development so much less phenomenal.

IV. MESSIANIC

1. There are direct prophecies of Christ, increasing in clearness: (a) The Woman's Seed (Gen. 3:15); (b) Abraham's Seed (Gen. 22:16); (c) Shiloh of Judah (Gen. 49:10); (d) The Passover Lamb (Exod. 12); (e) The Star and Scepter (Num. 24:17); (f) The Prophet (Deut. 18:15).

2. There are prophetic types: (a) Adam (Gen. 2 to 5; cf. 1 Cor. 15:45); (b) Abel (Gen. 4; cf. Heb. 12:24); (c) The Scapegoat (Lev. 16; cf. Heb. 9, 10); (d) The Red Heifer (Num. 19; cf. Heb. 9:13); (e) The Brazen Serpent (Num. 21; cf. John 3:14).

3. There are typical scenes, characters and ordinances: Paradise, the Rainbow, the Ark, Sarah and Hagar, Isaac and Ishmael, Esau and Jacob, Circumcision, Sacrifices, the Tabernacle, the High Priesthood. (Cf. Rev. 2:7; 4:3; 11:19; Gal. 4:22-31; Rom. 9:6-13; Col. 2:11; and the Epistle to the Hebrews).

4. We have our Lord's own word for this aspect of the Pentateuch, when He said in referring to Moses, " — for he wrote of Me" (John 5:46; cf. 1:45).

V. Spiritual

1. There is Progressive Sequence: Human Failure, Genesis; Divine Redemption, Exodus; Worship and Holiness, Leviticus; Order and Guidance, Numbers; Preparation for Inheritance, Deuteronomy.

2. There are Great Principles: Ruin, Redemption, Religion, Removal, Repetition; Sin, Salvation, Separation, Sanctification, Service.

3. There is Experimental Growth: Man's Condition leads to God's Provision — Access, Progress, Fulness of Blessing.

It has been said regarding these five great Books:

In Genesis God selects a field in which to sow the seed of His law; that field, of course, is the Israelitish nation. In Exodus He purchases and secures the field. In Leviticus He brings forth His seed, but finds the ground hard and thorny. In Numbers, for forty years, He is ploughing, clearing, and preparing the field; and in Deuteronomy He is again sowing the seed and harrowing it in.

Many of these truths find their parallel New Testament expression in the Epistle to the Romans. Cf. in particular 1:1, 2; 3:21; the main thesis of the Book, to 11:36; and 16:25-27.[1]

---

1. For detailed treatment see the author's volume, *St. Paul's Epistle to the Romans — A Devotional Commentary* (Wm. B. Eerdmans Publishing Co., 1945).